OCD AND MARRIAGE

Pathways to Reshaping Your Lives Together

By
David T. Culkin, PhD
Michaela A. Culkin, PhD

T0164074

Specialty Press, Inc.
3150 Willow Lane
Weston, Florida 33331

Book Design and Layout: Holly A. Carroll

Specialty Press, Inc.
3150 Willow Lane
Weston, Florida 33331
(954) 412-1332 (P) • (954) 206-6955 (Fax)

Printed in the United States of America.
ISBN 9781937761295
Library of Congress Control Number: 2021941931

Dedication

To our parents and mental health
professionals, who gave us the
tools to strengthen and flourish
in our marriage over the years.
We are forever grateful.

Pax

Acknowledgments

We are very grateful to the many people who have supported us over the years to achieve this milestone. First, our parents and immediate family members—past and present— have been there our entire journey. Next, our health care providers, particularly Dr. Jacqueline Pfeiffer who diagnosed us, retain a special place in our marriage. Also, we owe an enormous debt to our spiritual directors—willing and unwilling, alive and deceased, real and imagined. Without these supporters, we would not be here today. Finally, a special note of thanks to Dr. Harvey Parker and Melissa Orlov who advised us along the way. To all, many sincere thanks.

Contents

Foreword

Since I first learned about OCD as a college student, I have been fascinated with learning more about it and how to help people afflicted with it. People with OCD experience senseless yet distressing intrusive thoughts, ideas, and images—that same thoughts that everyone else experiences. Yet in OCD they provoke intense anxiety, guilt, and other forms of distress, along with urges to respond by engaging in avoidance and often elaborate compulsive rituals to try to control or reduce this distress, get rid of the thoughts, and prevent feared outcomes from taking place. But as much as these strategies seem like the best way to handle intrusive thoughts, they end up backfiring and leading to even more obsessional thoughts and anxiety. That is the vicious cycle of OCD, and as you probably know, it's difficult to get out of without professional help. If you've picked up this book, you're probably also aware that people with OCD may go to great lengths to structure their environment to minimize obsessional thoughts. But it is precisely this that keeps them from recognizing that obsessional thoughts are safe and not worth the time and energy people with OCD believe they must invest in controlling them.

We have some very effective treatments for OCD. Many people respond well to certain types of medications, for example. But my reading of the scientific literature suggests that we get the biggest bang for our buck from a certain form of cognitive-behavior therapy (CBT) called exposure and response prevention (or ERP). ERP teaches people skills for responding differently when obsessional thoughts and compulsive urges show up, even though ERP is the best treatment we've got, it is true that not everyone responds. I, for example, have received years of world-class training from some of the best minds in the field of OCD and worked with hundreds if not thousands of patients; but even so, not all of them get better. And so I've dedicated my career as a psychological researcher to trying to figure out what factors predict a desirable versus an undesirable outcome.

In 2006 I relocated from the Mayo Clinic to the University of North Carolina at Chapel Hill. When I did so, I began collaborating with Dr. Donald Baucom, another professor at Carolina and one of the world's experts in the field of interpersonal relationships. Dr. Baucom and I received a grant from the International OCD Foundation (IOCDF) to develop and evaluate a treatment program for couples affected by OCD. I didn't realize it at the time, but of all the studies my team has conducted over the years, this research (which continues to this day) has had the greatest impact on my clinical work with OCD patients. Expanding my understanding of the interpersonal aspects of OCD has taken my work as a clinician to a whole new level. Whereas I once felt it was sometimes important to involve family members when treating someone with OCD, I now view this as essential. I consider OCD a "family affair," and as part of therapy I teach partners and family members how to do their part to properly support their loved one while also keeping their family in balance.

That's where this fantastic book by Drs. David and Michaela Culkin comes in. Using their first-hand knowledge of OCD and marriage, they have combined their own personal experience with the state-of-the art scientific research to write an extremely useful guide for couples navigating the "OCD waters." Crucially, they emphasize what I believe are the two most significant issues when treading in these waters: good communication with your partner and reducing accommodation of the OCD symptoms. But this book covers a range of other important topics as well: learning about how OCD works, how it's treated, and how to fill in the gaps in a relationship that are left behind once OCD is out of the picture. Speaking of gaps, even though many people with OCD are in intimate relationships, resources for couples dealing with OCD are few and far between. This terrific book certainly helps to fill that gap!

Jonathan Abramowitz, PhD, Chapel Hill, North Carolina

What others say

" *Using their first-hand knowledge of OCD and marriage, they (David and Michaela Culkin) have combined their own personal experience with the state-of-the art scientific research to write an extremely useful guide for couples navigating the "OCD waters."*

– Jonathan Abramowitz, PhD, Chapel Hill, North Carolina

" *I will never forget the day that I asked Dave to consider writing a book on obsessive-compulsive disorder (OCD) and the effects on marriage. I told him, "You and Michaela have quite a success story to tell." We spent several sessions discussing how the book might be best formed. We imagined that Dave would capitalize on his amazing artistic talents and Michaela would utilize her years of leadership and teaching experience. What has resulted is this fantastic literary work which guides couples to a greater understanding of OCD and a method to navigate through marital life and unifying love.*

It is a double win for the Culkin marital team because each partner contributes to the mapping and strategic planning for the adventures in marriage. Dave and Michaela both enjoy traveling so they use this theme throughout the book. It has been a prosperous and exciting time to see each spouse grow in acceptance and understanding of OCD and to merge their perspectives in order to help others in their lives.

I am proud to know and acknowledge Dave and Michaela Culkin as a couple who seek a greater good for themselves and others by bringing understanding, compromise, and collaboration to a subject matter that needs to be addressed."

– Jacqueline R. Pfeifer, PhD

❝ *The Culkins have provided the gift of hope and a way out of the confusion and struggles experienced by couples impacted by OCD. You are not alone, and OCD and Marriage deftly illuminates the paths that can lead to a happier, healthier life together."*

    – Melissa Orlov, founder of adhdmarriage.com, and author of *The ADHD Effect on Marriage and The Couple's Guide to Thriving with ADHD*

❝ *David and Michaela Culkin have created a much needed resource for gaining insights and healing a marriage where one or both partners suffer with OCD. As they each reveal their life stories, the reader begins to identify deeply with the distress created by obsessive compulsive disorder. OCD and Marriage: Pathways to Reshaping Your Lives Together encourages the reader to "let go of" the traps which have led to disappointment and disillusionment in the relationship with one's self, a spouse, and OCD. The reader discovers new tools for collaborating with one's spouse and building a firm foundation to promote a greater sense of unity. Gaining awareness is often a catalyst for change. However, the Culkins remove the focus from encouraging minor improvements and adjustments which are frequently recommended by mental health professionals because those adjustments do not impact the core of the marital relationship experiencing the presence of OCD. Instead, The 6-Pathway Model is provided to shift the focus to permanent change, growth, and healing of each individual and the marriage. The Model provides multidimensional insights and guidelines for creating a new way of perceiving what has and is taking place in the relationship with Self and one's spouse. Compassion and empathy replace frustration, impatience, shame, and the sense of hopelessness with a new vision for what is possible in marriage . . . with or without OCD."*

    – Janet A. Beverley, LSCSW, Psychotherapist, Consultant, and author of *Creating Loving Relationships: Living a Life of Authenticity*

Preface

The global epidemic of anxiety and obsessive-compulsive related disorders has risen to levels that threaten the happiness, well-being, and sanity of more people than ever before. These disorders that bring about phobias, doubts, and uncertainty can efficiently and effectively infect and destroy the lives of individuals and their families regardless of nationality, age, gender, or any other background. Fortunately, there has been research on ways to help people who are affected by disorders through medication and therapy. This book has been written to add to the knowledge base, and it aims to help those who suffer through the daily effects of obsessive-compulsive disorder (OCD) on marriages and long-term partnerships. This book takes a unique look at how partners of any background can work together by learning from our experiences and available research to cope with a disorder that brings anxiety and hysteria and replaces it with peace, listening, and healing.

This book is *for survivors by survivors* **of OCD.** We stress "survivors" from the perspective of a couple who has learned to move forward in a healthy way, despite the difficulties OCD brings to a relationship. This has been a journey for us, and while we may never be completely healed from the effects of OCD, we have constantly worked together to live our lives as we choose, not as OCD dictates. We are not writing this book as an all-encompassing solution but instead as a workbook in which you can learn from our failures and successes. For those who have been diagnosed and continue to struggle with the daily, sometimes stealthy, anguish caused by this disease, we—as authors, spouses, and survivors—have literally felt and dealt with your pain. We have written about our experiences to remind readers and fellow sufferers, including ourselves, that we are not alone. It is our intent to help not only the people who struggle with OCD, but also the family members and health care providers who assist them. Therapists may find the text useful as a guide for counseling couples with the disorder. This book includes some of our most vulnerable experiences, offering a view of the disorder from within.

Our goal of this book is simple: by telling our story, we can continue to heal while helping others who are in different parts along their journey. **OCD does not and will not be allowed to take over a marriage.** We have spent plenty of time in mental health offices to address our unique set of symptoms, OCD, and its effect on our marriage. Together we are a force that cannot only survive OCD, but also take on any challenge and be better and stronger for the effort. Using the strength we have developed over numerous years, we intend for this book to do the following: encourage individuals diagnosed with OCD to face the disorder head-on together with their partners, assist couples in reaching out for support in the community, and seek relationship-based healing that works with established, evidence-based therapies.

This book provides a new perspective on OCD treatment and survival from the stance of the patient and partner. Rather than approach coping with OCD from a clinical perspective, we offer sufferers and their partners a resource we wished we had when we struggled with the myths, barriers, and threats of the disorder. Central to this is a focus on strengthening marital relationships through active, creative communication. This focus on communication highlights our belief that living with OCD is a family affair by which everyone affected—whether care giver or sufferer—is a survivor. By sharing our own experiences of grief, fear of the unknown, and humor, we invite others to re-story their roles and expectations towards empowerment. As non-therapists who have dedicated our professional lives to educating others, we survey an overlooked element of living with OCD: learning to better ourselves by crafting our own life stories of survival. We also provide stories and convey messages in various forms to target a spectrum of ages and learning styles. As a result, we hope to achieve these aims and help others to strengthen relationships with themselves, communities, and society.

This workbook uses memories of our experiences as a diagnosed individual and a spouse-caregiver to achieve the goals listed above. To achieve these goals, we have written chapters from survivors' points of view to encourage you to seek help and author OCD's role in your relationship. Chapters are organized according to experiences with living with OCD in a marriage and aim to give practical examples to combat everyday challenges. This book's structure is flexible enough to address pertinent coping issues while allowing for the appropriate injection of humor and varied perspectives that appeal to a broad audience. After all, OCD does not distinguish its victims, and we choose not to limit our message to "typical" audiences.

David & Michaela

Authors' Note

We chose to tell our story from our perspective in order to share our experiences empathetically with those open enough to hear them. To protect our privacy while providing material with which readers can resonate, we have provided several of our personal experiences living with OCD—not all. In many sections, David is the narrator unless Michaela explicitly identifies herself. By speaking mostly in first person, we could convey more effectively our constructed meanings and vulnerabilities while modeling a personal narrative which readers experiencing many of the same feelings and challenges could embrace and make their own.

Where possible, we also use alternate genders of personal pronouns to be as inclusive as possible. If masculine gender is used, it does not exclude feminine or non-binary possibilities—and vice versa. We intend to respect all readers who choose other personal pronouns for identification. Furthermore, we focus on married couples and do not discriminate between heterosexual and non-binary unions.

We acknowledge Melissa Orlov's (2010) 6–Step Model for attention deficit hyperactivity disorder (ADHD) which we have adapted for conditions unique to OCD. We configured the model, with her permission, to be non-sequential among its six elements. This allowed us to describe the disruptive nature of OCD while providing readers with enough flexibility to confront the disorder in their own ways, with their own voices. Orlov's Model has been extremely effective for ADHD sufferers, and we saw how it can immensely help couples cope with OCD.

There are several texts mentioned throughout this book that address OCD in families, general relationships, and individuals. While we address some aspects of OCD related to marriage such as OCD in families, comorbidities, etc., we also recognize the numerous resources already available on these subjects. Because of this, we have chosen to acknowledge these topics while concentrating on the purpose of this book: OCD in marriage and long-term partnerships.[1]

1. Check out our website ocdandmarriage.com for more information and resources.

How to Use This Book

Readers may read the chapters and sections sequentially to get a holistic approach to OCD in marriage. The chapters are designed to build upon each other, inviting readers to interact with the material in a logical flow. Those who would like to concentrate on specific topics may consider reading our personal experiences in Section I or available resources and tools in Section III. Finally, therapists and caregivers may find the 6-Pathway Model description along with the interactive exercises in Section II effective ways to focus therapy sessions.

Understanding
OCD
in Your Marriage

Key Objectives

This section intends to help you:

- know us through our personal story of living with OCD

- better understand OCD as a neuropsychiatric disorder

- identify key elements of a good marriage

- become more aware of this disorder and its impact on marital relationships

- define and identify OCD within the context of your family

- know that survivors are not alone

- better understand available treatments for the disorder

Chapter 1

Our Stories

Life with OCD is a journey,
that never ends; constantly casts doubt
over home base and destination,
over security and insecurity,
between lovers and caregivers,
between isolation and time out,
amidst perseveration and impatience,
cloaked within a mask of self-centeredness.
—David Culkin, July 5, 2017

Marriage, Family, and OCD

Marriage is complex enough without obsessive-compulsive disorder (OCD). Marriage is not for the complacent; it takes a lot of work, communication, and trust. Undiagnosed OCD, in particular, causes even more pain and struggle above and beyond a typical marriage. This book cuts through this complexity and focuses on both partners affected by OCD while offering fundamental ways to develop and strengthen the marriage. This book is recommended for couples who are committed to working together along with their therapists. Following this intent should help all stakeholders to navigate the journey of healing—to learn how to thrive while combating OCD.

Our Experience

The following story describes our married OCD experience by illustrating key concepts addressed throughout this book. While you read along, consider how your own experiences mirror or differ from ours and how that informs the level of awareness of your own situation.

David's Story

One of my earliest OCD memories was from third grade. My parents had just divorced, and my mother had moved my brother and me to a new town. New school. New friends. New everything. I thought I was going with the flow—but I wasn't. Then the teacher assigned a bunch of homework. I couldn't explain it, but I was so overwhelmed because I knew not only that I had to complete these tasks but perform them perfectly. I feared I didn't have the capacity to do the work without mistakes in such a short time. I didn't have the words to explain to my mom why I felt inundated, so I just looked at her and cried.[2] Even then, I knew somewhere in the back of my head that I was overreacting, that I would work through it. After all, I'd always been a hard worker. Only looking back decades later could I perceive the trigger event and a call for help that I could only make by crying. Many events such as this occurred during my formative years, marking a path of obsessive-compulsive cycles that I could only perceive much later. It wasn't until my life partner pointed out some of these instances that I could more clearly analyze the OCD in my life.

Michaela and I met over twenty-five years ago at a college football game. I was an usher for a local church group, and she was attending the game. I didn't think much of the encounter at the time and did not realize how that chance meeting would affect my life. Over the next few years, we kept in touch and became close friends. As Michaela

---

2. Sometimes I encounter children who may exhibit obsessive-compulsive traits. I'm not a clinician, but we all act compulsively sometimes. The difference for children is that they sometimes do not possess the communication skills to express specific indicators of their distress (APA, 2013a, 2013b), leaving parents and educators to infer root causes.

pursued more educational opportunities in another state, we continued to communicate and support each other: I by listening to her daily successes and challenges and she by writing letters of support as I traveled with my career. We both, through our developing relationship, found solace in our friendship and natural comfort in each other's presence. This relationship began to blossom into love. After a year-long engagement, we were married at the same church we attended after we met—just in time for the military to move us to another part of the country.

Life as a newly married couple can be tumultuous and frenetic at times, perhaps explaining why it was difficult to discern the gradual toll my OCD was taking on the marriage. We experienced the usual disagreements and negotiations every couple faces when learning to live together. Despite this, we began to feel something was off. Perhaps it was the psychologist who handed me a pamphlet on OCD medications during a follow-up appointment for Michaela when she described my intrusive thoughts. Maybe it was the very detailed briefs during which I demanded that Michaela focus in absolute attention to my daily activities and inadequacies. After all, who better than my best friend to absorb and fix my problems? Or was it spontaneous public prayers when I placed my hands on her head to bless her from whatever force might hurt her at any given moment? At the very least, she would thank me for protecting her…or so I thought.

By year seven of our marriage, it was obvious to both of us that my "uncommanded thoughts," as we called them, were growing more frequent and more disruptive of the normal routines of our lives. I also found that any event that disrupted my normal routine or schedule would set me on an anxiety-ridden cycle that made me feel rigid and unsettled. It wasn't OK when I was rude to family and friends when they visited us and disrupted my routine. I knew it was not normal for the violent, sexual, and taboo thoughts to take over my confidence, incessantly fueling fear of further uncertainty. *Was I capable of doing those things? Was I a bad person because they entered my mind?* Although I knew I would not carry out these deluded thoughts that kept cycling in my mind, I constantly asked Michaela for assurance: "Will I be OK? I'm not going to hurt you, am I?" She once responded with an insight that I still cherish: "Dave, you worry about things you won't do; there are people out there who don't worry about what they've done." I felt broken and we knew I needed help.

Not knowing the real cause of my mental unease, we sought answers through more traditional means. We attended a church-sponsored marriage enrichment kayak trip, meant to give couples an opportunity to work together while navigating a river and discuss topics related to marriage. (We quickly learned that while we were able to discuss pertinent parts of our relationship with ease, we needed our own kayak as we were both headstrong paddlers and navigators.) We attended a series of counseling sessions targeted on helping our marriage, but we felt at a loss because we communicated well and shared the load. We learned that we each needed our own counseling sessions and that the general marriage counseling was not helping our relationship. We didn't realize that we were really wrestling with OCD—related challenges. We needed to do something beyond just talking about our woes.

Seeking others who were going through similar situations, we attended group marital-support sessions which provided us tools for conflict resolution. What we didn't realize was our challenges went beyond typical conflict resolution in a relationship. While we still felt there was a hole that wasn't being filled in our relationship, we did discover one tool that helped in public situations when I began to feel anxious, squeezing each other's hands three times became an intimate way to say, "I-love-you" in public. This became a secret signal between the two of us that everything *was* OK and *would be* OK, no matter the social situation. (We still do this silent, sacred code in uneasy situations, and find it just as intimate almost twenty years later.) As a result, we gradually became increasingly aware that remedies sought by "typical" couples weren't addressing our unique needs—something was still missing. If we didn't seek help to address the unknown gap in our relationship, we both knew the marriage wouldn't last.

Our decision to seek professional psychological therapy helped to save our marriage, that is one thing of which I can be certain. The biggest hurdle was to get past the social stigma of seeking professional help. We chose a psychologist who was not affiliated with my job, so I would not have to worry about being exposed as weak to people in my immediate circle at work or—worse yet—lose any of the roles of my job that I had worked so hard to attain. In short, a lot was on the line: my marriage, career track, and sanity. We both knew that the "hole" in our marriage was greater than communication issues; there had to be something more that was acting as an opposing force. We were at a fork in the journey of mental illness, and we chose psychological treatment.

Fortunately, during these sessions I had enough self-awareness that I could describe my thought processes when I would obsessively cycle on sexual-violent thoughts (*Will I stab my wife? Will I run away with that attractive woman?*) and checking (*I think I locked that door*) or scrupulosity (*I have prayed the Hail Mary five times without interruption to "make it count"*). It seemed like I was always trying to wrestle with whether or not I was a good person because of the thoughts I was having. Within two sessions, the clinician began focusing on my incessant thoughts and my reluctance to reveal my vulnerabilities. By the third or so session, she asked if anyone had ever suggested OCD to me *because I had it*. That diagnosis was a life-changing moment in our relationship.

Almost twenty years after that revelation, Michaela and I have survived and have strengthened our relationship. The severity and length of time I have exhibited symptoms may mean I have to take medications for the rest of my life. However, knowing the root cause of many of our challenges was freedom because we could finally name and study our opponent. We could research the disorder, find support groups and organizations, and seek therapy (both cognitive-behavioral therapy and medications). For us, the alternative of divorce was never an option.

Michaela's Story

"I'm *SO* OCD." This can be heard on any given day in our society, whether in conversation, in the things we watch on TV, or in social media. This phrase can be uttered in a joking way to illustrate a person's need to have everything in order. Most people who say this equate OCD with keeping things in perfect order or to planning a schedule that accounts for every minute of the day—hence the saying that has been disseminated in popular culture—*"I'm so OCD, I have CDO."* By ordering the letters of OCD in alphabetical order, the person is illustrating the need to have everything lined up and in a certain order. These are more perfectionist tendencies, and less about OCD. This phrase can be seen on magnets, mugs, and t-shirts. OCD's cultural popularity does not reflect the reality of its destructive effects on married life.

When people refer to OCD in stereotypes, they can diminish the very real pain of this psychiatric disorder—a disorder that goes beyond personality traits and can destroy relationships. As a spouse/caregiver to someone with OCD, I cringe when I hear people make light of OCD. While I know most of the time the phrase is said without a second thought and in a joking manner without thinking of those who live daily with the mental disorder, I often wonder if people would be so quick to tease if they *truly* knew what living with OCD (either as one who suffers or a family member) was really like. The reality is, teasing that a person has OCD can inadvertently diminish the experience a person and their partner has with OCD. It is one thing to have traits of OCD, but the reality is that a diagnosis of the illness can cause extreme anxiety—nobody *wants* OCD. When OCD is trivialized as a disorder that is used as an adjective or verb when talking about personal character traits, it can diminish the pain that the illness can instill within a relationship.

While I can't be *IN* my husband's brain to empathize with the pain and uncertainty of uncommanded obsessive thoughts and compulsions, I can sympathize as a caregiver who lives in the wake of

OCD day after day. The best way I can explain it as a caretaker is that OCD is like living with two different people and dealing with each person in a different way. The person I married is a caring, loving, humorous man who would do anything for me. "Herb," as we call the OCD, is selfish, looking out for himself and his instant gratification as he carries out compulsions or perseverates over intrusive thoughts. I can be myself around Dave, but I have to tiptoe gently around Herb.

Since the diagnosis of OCD didn't enter our life until we had been married for seven years, we automatically assumed it was us. We sought marriage counseling, couple's therapy, self-help books...none of it really rang true to the reality of our situation. Only when we heard the diagnosis from our therapist, "It sounds like OCD," did we have a pivot point to delve into a category of mental illness that we hadn't even thought to consider. We researched OCD, we sought couple's therapy to learn to live with our new diagnosis, and we attended individual therapy sessions. We even drove an hour to attend a support group for those with OCD. We found there was a lot of information about therapy for those who suffer with OCD—from cognitive-behavioral therapy (CBT), including exposure and response prevention, to medications that would help to lessen the heavy load of OCD's effect on the brain. What we had a difficult time with was finding support groups or literature to assist caretakers who lived with OCD every day. As a result, we decided to write a book with the outcome of helping couples who would find themselves in a similar situation to ours.

This book is not the "be all, end all." It is not written from a therapist's point of view. Instead, it is written by a couple who experiences the daily effects of OCD in their relationship. Our journey has not been easy. It has taken a lot of time to arrive where we are today. It is our goal to let you, the reader, know you are not alone in this journey, and with hard work and dedication, you and your partner can filter out the haze and uncertainty of OCD from your relationship, leaving a clearer view of who your partner is who is carrying the load of OCD every day. As partners, you can bear that load together.

Chapter 2
What Makes a Good Marriage?

Before we begin to talk about OCD and its effects on marriage, it's important to define the essential ingredients in a strong marriage, regardless of whether or not OCD plays a critical role. In 2019, there were approximately 2 million couples[3] who got married in the United States. Many of these relationships begin with romantic love that is more passionate and physical. How can a couple strengthen that love to become more selfless, unconditional, and enduring? How can a relationship mature and develop over a long period of time? Life Innovations surveyed 21,501 married couples in all 50 states to determine the top 10 strengths and stumbling blocks of marriages. By identifying the top 10 strengths of happy marriages, the researchers were able to identify the happy and unhappy marriages with 93% accuracy.[4]

---

3. See https://www.cdc.gov/nchs/fastats/marriage-divorce.htm.
4. See firstthings.org/building-a-strong-marriage/ for more details on strengths and problems in marriages.

Top 10 Strengths of Happy Marriages

1. Partners are satisfied with how each person talks to the other.
2. Partners are creative in handling differences.
3. They feel close to one another.
4. Neither partner is too controlling.
5. When discussing problems, partners understand each other's opinions and ideas.
6. Partners are satisfied with the amount of affection shown and received.
7. There is a good balance of leisure time spent together and separately.
8. Friends and family rarely interfere with the relationship.
9. Partners agree on how to spend money.
10. They are satisfied with how each other expresses spiritual values and beliefs.

The results of the survey also identified that the strongest marriages are those where partners have strong communication skills, show flexibility, are close to one another, and have compatible personalities to help resolve conflicts.

Communication Skills

Those in happy marriages report they feel understood by their partners and find it easier to share their feelings with one another, especially when their partner doesn't use put-downs. Partners in happy marriages are six times more likely than their counterparts to agree that they are satisfied with how they talk to one another. Happy couples report they feel understood by their partners and can share their feelings, especially during a disagreement.

Listening is crucial to a happy marriage since it is more about trying to understand one another instead of spending energy on judgment. Conflicts, when handled in a healthy way, can benefit a relationship and help couples come to a resolution. Seventy-eight percent of happy couples in the survey agreed that they were creative when handling differences between one another.

Conflict is inevitable in human relationships. There will always be differences between people, sometimes ending in disagreements. The survey of marital strengths found that most happy couples feel their conflicts are resolved, and disagreements are less about placing blame and more about finding common ground. As a result, similar conflict resolution skills are of the utmost importance in a strong and happy relationship.

Couple Flexibility

Flexibility, as defined by the survey results, refers to how open couples are to change in their marriages. Flexibility helps couples to manage daily stressors and maintain an openness to change, regardless of cultural norms. Partners in a happy relationship are willing to move away from the more traditional roles and adjust as needed when running errands, completing household chores, and cooking.

Couples in the survey shared they were happier and more satisfied when household chores were divided amongst the two partners. Happy couples reported they weren't as concerned about who was doing more of the share of the daily tasks and worked to maintain an equal relationship.

Closeness

You feel close to your partner when you are emotionally connected to him or her. Closeness also includes a balance of together time and separate time. Happy couples who feel emotionally connected are open to asking for help from one another and enjoy spending time with one another.

Compatible Personalities

Partners in happy marriages reported to have personalities that complement one another. They build on each other's strengths and address differences creatively to work together for the best interest of the marriage. When partners share goals for the relationship, they tend to forge a stronger bond.

Top 10 Problems in Marriages

The survey identified ten predominant problems in unhappy marriages. Review this list below and consider which items resonate with your relationship.

Table 2.1

YES	NO	Identified Issue
		1. We have problems sharing leadership.
		2. One of us is too stubborn.
		3. There is stress created by how to raise a child based on how one of us was raised.
		4. One of us is too negative or critical.
		5. One of us feels responsible for the issues in the marriage.
		6. One of us wishes the other had more time to share.
		7. There is an avoidance of conflict.
		8. One of us wishes the other was more willing to share feelings.
		9. There is a difficulty completing daily tasks in the marriage.
		10. Differences between partners are not resolved.

Interestingly enough, when reflecting on the first years of our marriage, we see that most of our problems fit in the "Top 10 Problems in Marriages." It wasn't until we identified the problems related to OCD and addressed them head-on that we began to move more towards the "Top Ten Strengths of a Happy Marriage." You will find many challenges in a marriage, but the challenges of OCD add another complete layer of difficulty.

The Bank of Civility

In every relationship, there are consequences for every action. These consequences may be negative resulting in a loss of trust, or positive resulting in enhanced feelings of love. These results stem from the choices we make. We all make choices. That's where the bank of civility comes into play.

The bank of civility is a metaphor for the repository of feelings in a relationship. When a partner chooses to invest in the relationship by complimenting or being courteous to their partner, a deposit is made. Likewise, the partner who chooses to swear at the other partner and take the person for granted makes a withdrawal. Overall, it is the choice and action of being taken for granted that hurts the couple because neither partner will have access to the investment that could have been deposited. Put another way, either partner can make a withdrawal from a lifetime of positive, life-affirming investments. Love has an ineffable way of providing infinite rates of interest in any relationship.

How can you work together to build your own investment? It can be little things such as saying thank you to one another for even the smallest things, like passing the salt at dinner. A person may feel it is a bit silly to follow such chivalry, but it is a way to constantly remind each other that they are present to one another. Unexpectedly, this sense of a partner's value can increase over the years with events that remind us of life's frailty—death of friends, parents who have cancer, heavy life events, etc. Death has a way of putting perspective on life. At the same time, depositing positivity in the bank often extends beyond simple courtesies. Sometimes, partners must do the most difficult things (such as apologize or forgive) to deepen the relationship. Much like a charity donation fund, partners must constantly look for opportunities to donate their resources (like love, time, and trust) to develop a worthy cause such as the relationship.

How do you invest in your bank? Maybe it is time to build up some relationship capital. We have found this especially important in a marriage that also has an OCD component.

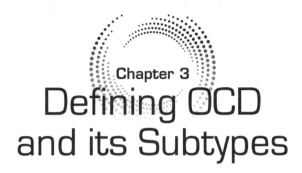

Chapter 3
Defining OCD and its Subtypes

What is OCD?

Obsessive-compulsive disorder (OCD) belongs to a family of related disorders grounded in a baseline of anxiety induced by a fear of uncertainty. According to the *Diagnostic and Statistical Manual of Mental Disorders* (DSM-5),[5] OCD particularly involves "obsessive preoccupation and repetitive behaviors [or compulsions]" that can overwhelm one's daily life. OCD is not just a trait or a perfectionist tendency that many of us have in certain areas of our lives. Those may be indicators of a larger problem or just a personality quirk. Neither does the disorder discriminate between race, religion, gender, sexual orientation, nor socioeconomic background; it is an equal-opportunity predator. What separates OCD as a disorder is the harmful and detrimental effect it has on personal relationships over time. As illustrated in our married experience and for the purpose of this book,

5. See American Psychiatric Association (APA) DSM-5 (APA, 2013b; see also APA, 2013a).

OCD is a neuropsychiatric disorder that is believed to involve biochemical imbalances and genetic predispositions that, when triggered, can result in persistent obsessive fears that may be temporarily relieved by repetitive compulsive behaviors or mental actions that negatively affect a marriage.[6] It impairs life and prevents us from enjoying daily experiences with loved ones.

All people have intrusive thoughts from one time to another—it's a normal part of life. We all worry about loved ones and their safety, what the future holds, and other typical life events. A diagnosis of OCD is made when the intrusive thoughts take over the typical routines in a person's life, taking more time than is normal, causing significant anxiety, or interfering with daily functions and relationships. Obsessive thoughts and ritualistic compulsions that take time and energy away from living a typical life are hallmarks of OCD.

Obsessive thoughts can cause an unhealthy fear of germs, contracting a disease, or being hurt. Compulsions can include routine, daily tasks like checking on things such as the stove or door locks, cleaning things over and over to prevent contamination, or hand washing to prevent germs from making a person sick. Obsessions and compulsions don't necessarily link to what one would think of as typical cause and effect. For example, a person may think they have to say a certain word or count to a certain number; otherwise, a family member will get sick.

The majority of people who have OCD can function in daily life without detection of the OCD. While some of our friends think David has his quirky ways, it wasn't until we talked about his OCD that they realized he had a mental disorder that affected our daily routines.

---

6. See the DSM-5 for an array of symptoms, treatments, and levels of insight that apply to this incurable disorder but are beyond this book's scope (APA, 2013a).

Why is OCD a Disorder?

The dictionary definition of *disorder* is a state of confusion or chaos. We are often confused and find ourselves challenged by circumstances that go beyond our immediate abilities to deal with them. Married people dealing with OCD can easily feel overwhelmed by a lack of control and fear of uncertainty on a daily basis. In this sense, *disorder* aptly describes the persistent effect of OCD on a marriage and its members.

OCD can impair daily functions. It is one thing to read about validated OCD symptoms and quite another to have lived your entire life with some of them without knowing they were evidence of a disorder. In my case, something was wrong and I didn't know it. For example, I had always found the concept of symmetry, equality and completeness of sizes and shapes and concepts very appealing. I would expend a lot of time and energy making sure my bed, books, and homework assignments were 'just right.' What I did not understand until I was married was that obsessions "...about symmetry can derail the timely completion of school or work projects (*for example, I was normally the last to leave the exam room*) because the project never feels 'just right,' potentially resulting in school failure or job loss."[7] While I never lost a job due to OCD, I did stay up until 2 a.m. many evenings during high school retyping (on my IBM Selectric) sections of biology reports just to make them whole and somehow perfect. This negative effect on daily actions had longer-term consequences for my ability to participate in mature relationships in both personal and professional environments.

To be sure, OCD can negatively impact relationships. The unbridled fear of uncertainty can often lead to the temptation to control everyday behaviors. When you control the behavior of your spouse, it can lead to problems. David Clark and Shelley Rhyno

7. APA, 2013a, p. 240.

(2005), writing about unwanted intrusive thoughts, explain it is the frequency and degree of uncontrolled thoughts that set those with a disorder apart from the general population. *The Diagnostic and Statistical Manual of Mental Disorders* (DSM-5) further notes that"…some individuals with OCD try to impose rules and prohibitions on family members because of their disorder (no one in the family can have visitors to the house for fear of contamination), and this can lead to family dysfunction."[8] My daily briefs to Michaela, especially during the early years of our marriage before I was treated, exemplify this phenomenon. I would psychologically hold her hostage when I returned home from work while I reported out to her the details of my days. While this compulsion made sense to me (*after all, I was communicating everything I could so I could save our marriage*), I only realized the abnormality of it when such behavior threatened our marriage.

Disorders are not necessarily characterized by stereotypes. Stereotypes are cultural ideals, images of what most would think about a concept. The popular concept of OCD often conjures perfection, concern, and excessive cleaning. These characteristics certainly are some descriptors of the disorder in diagnostic manuals used by clinicians. But popular stereotypes often miss the shadows of OCD, the ones that really hurt marriages. The basic criteria for OCD symptoms include the "presence of obsessions and compulsions" which are "time-consuming (e.g., more than 1 hour per day) or cause clinically significant distress or impairment to warrant a diagnosis of OCD."[9] People who live with OCD are very aware that something is off, even if they cannot explicitly describe it. With good or fair insight into OCD, the "individual recognizes that obsessive-compulsive disorder beliefs are definitely or probably not true or that they may or may not be true."[10] In other words, the DSM-5 describes the disorder as a phenomenon that reduces the quality of life through an

8. APA, 2013a, p. 241.
9. APA, 2013a, p. 238.
10. APA, 2013a, p. 237.

impairment of daily functions based on the fear of uncertainty and lack of control over it.

Another attribute of disorders is that they like company. After all, chaos is more fun at a party than in your living room. The DSM-5 describes common instances of co-morbidities in which OCD can occur with other disorders such as depression, eating disorders, and personality disorders. For example, "Obsessive-compulsive personality disorder is not characterized by intrusive thoughts, images, or urges or by repetitive behaviors that are performed in response to these intrusions; instead, it involves an enduring and pervasive maladaptive pattern of excessive perfectionism and rigid control."[11] Clinicians will have to identify these comorbid disorders in order to treat them by priority.

In short, OCD is a disorder because it impairs daily functions to a degree and frequency that normally exceed what is considered normal for the general population. It is a fine-tuned machine of uncertainty that, left untreated or ignored, could reap untold harm on any marriage. Because OCD can invade any facet of a partnered relationship at any time, we'll describe the many subtypes of the disorder.

OCD Subtypes

To understand OCD as a mental disorder, it is critical to recognize that it can happen anywhere at any time. OCD is nuanced and can show up as a pesky obsession or energy-draining compulsion at the least expected moments. As our understanding of OCD's diversity has grown, psychologists have placed it into categories, or subtypes. Learning about these subtypes can help us to sympathize with those who suffer from obsessions and compulsions that differ from ours. While these categories are artificially defined, they can give us a sense of control over the nuanced situations in which OCD decides to show itself. In reality, the OCD experience can often be described along a

11. APA, 2013a, p. 242.

continuous spectrum, with a sufferer identifying more with some types than others depending upon circumstances of the moment (Clark, 2020). The categories can also help sufferers and caregivers appreciate that individuals can experience more than one type of subtype at different times in their lives. A consequence of this multiplicity is that types of OCD can affect our partners in different ways, meaning there may be different ways to handle them in relationships. Ultimately, living with and battling OCD can be exhausting for both partners in any relationship. Realizing that you have resources and that you are never alone is essential.

In this section, we'll identify commonly accepted OCD subtypes, how they can manifest in partnerships, and strategies to remedy the various symptoms.[12]

Contamination OCD Subtype

Has the thought of bodily fluids or unseen germs gripped you so much that you could not think of anything else? Have you feared that others might infect you, or you others? Such a sense of disgust for things that could possibly harm us is the foundation of Contamination OCD.

An interesting characteristic of contamination obsessions is that sufferers often know their fears are irrational. A dog owner may be a germaphobe and protect herself by always wearing gloves, double washing her hands, and carrying hand sanitizer with her at all times. But when she gets home, she lets her pet—whose nose has been who knows where—lick her face up and down for the nightly greeting.

With Contamination OCD, the obsession of somehow losing control in an invisible war against germs is non-stop. The fears may

---

12. We used David Clark's (2020) *Cognitive-Behavioral Therapy for OCD and Its Subtypes* as the baseline for the subtypes. Other authors may identify other subtypes, but we found these four are adequate to address the many faces of OCD and thus the many ways to confront them in relationships. Additional sources for targeting therapies include Jonathan Abramowitz's *Getting Over OCD* (2018) and *The Family Guide to Getting Over OCD* (2021). BeyondOCD.org also presents a comprehensive repository of tools and resources to learn more about OCD and to live with it.

stem from bodily fluids and excretions, infection of loved ones, or unseen viruses. The emotional response of disgust to this perceived loss of control can result in many forms of obsessions.

These obsessions can become cyclic thought patterns that are hard to stop. What if I have a disease that spreads to my wife? Do I want to infect her? What if others contaminate my drinking water? A cycle can snowball from seemingly harmless events. If I picked up this dirty glass without gloves, should I sanitize all my glasses to be sure I'm not responsible for infecting anyone else?

...a sense of disgust for things that could possibly harm us is the foundation of Contamination OCD.

As the obsessions cascade into greater fears, compulsive rituals may seem to be the only way to gain relief. Excessive cleaning rituals are common because they are simple. It's also easy to recruit loved ones to facilitate them. For example, a man who showers believes he can only use the soap bar once to ensure it doesn't collect germs when he's not around to ensure it remains clean. As a result of this irrational fear, he feels compelled to conduct a ritual whereby he uses the entire bar or bottle of body wash for each shower. Afterwards, it stands to reason that he must employ his partner to help him sanitize the shower and the surrounding bathroom to help ensure nothing else could contaminate the shower 'safe' space. The next time he showers, regardless of who has used it since, he must go through the same obsessive cycle and compulsive ritual. Understandably, this can be exhausting. It can make one want to avoid contaminants in the first place. Hence, avoidance is another common strategy to deal with contamination obsessions.

Contamination OCD has a prominent place in OCD cultural stereotypes. Movies about Howard Hughes and stories of famous people who don't shake hands are common. It can take a tremendous amount of mental and physical energy to address the fears that lead to intricate cognitive and cleaning rituals. Fear of uncertainty is at the root of Contamination OCD and other subtypes such as doubt and checking.

Doubt, Checking, and Repeating Subtype

A common theme in this subtype is doubt fostered by irrational perceptions or faulty reasoning (Clark, 2020). Sometimes known in the past as the 'doubting disease,' OCD does seem to thrive on fears of failure and uncertainty. These troublesome twins can lead a sufferer to convince herself that, somehow, "I'm responsible."

This overall sense of responsibility is often not grounded in reality, but in fear. For example, a non-OCD person may wonder once in a while whether they locked the car door in the parking lot of the train station. A person with OCD may start with the fear of losing the car. If the car is the family car, its loss may directly affect the family's livelihood and way of life. Furthermore, the person's partner may not be able to survive without the car (i.e., take kids to school, run errands, pay bills, etc.) and, left without any other choice, have to leave that person. Furthermore, there can be a strong emotional 'tag' attached to this cognitive cycle, leaving the person to think of nothing else but, "If I leave the car unlocked, I'll get divorced and lose my family." The person may realize this is irrational, but that knowledge doesn't reduce the emotional stress. A compulsive ritual—such as tapping the car three times with the keys, checking pockets for the keys every

> **This overall sense of responsiblity is often not grounded in reality, but in fear.**

10 feet, holding the keys so they are visible until sitting on the train with the doors closed—may seem to be the only way to get relief from the mental torture. This cyclic connection of faulty reasoning and short-term compulsions to somehow 'fix' a perceived problem is characteristic of this subtype.

This subtype may manifest itself in many ways. One of my earliest rituals I recall entailed me checking to make sure my school bag was zipped and secure every 30 feet or so. My fear was losing my textbooks, which were expensive. Cost is a big deal in a single-parent household. Somehow, I linked the possibility of an open bag—something we all do once in a while—to the perception that I would lose the textbooks and make my mother destitute. I illogically reasoned that over-checking was better than losing the house or my education. Other people experiencing this type of OCD may doubt their senses and repeatedly check or ask for reassurance. For instance, a person may listen to the police scanner every Monday to listen for any traffic incidents involving hit-and-runs during the weekend. No reports may temporarily comfort the person to know they did not run over someone accidentally on Saturday or Sunday. Other people—I'm famous for this—continually ask their loved ones, "Am I a good person? Are we going to be alright?" The faulty doubt can stem from uncertainty and the need for reassurance. As I grew up, I found it very difficult to separate my unwanted thoughts from reality. If I had a thought about stabbing someone (and I could physically do it), it somehow meant I wanted to stab someone and that I was therefore a bad person. Despite never stabbing anyone, I constantly feared I could and was thus bad. I had to confess and seek reassurance. In such cases, subtypes such as repeating and checking can overlap with others such as with harm, sex, and scrupulosity.

Exposure and response prevention (ERP) along with cognitive-behavioral therapy and possibly medication can be appropriate therapies for this subtype. In my case, I had OCD for so long that it had networked throughout most of my doubts, fears, and uncertainties. I will probably rely on medications for the rest of my life. That said, it was ERP that enabled me to convert the loud roars of obsessive thoughts into muddled humming. By regularly listening to recordings I made of my fears and possible strings of consequences, no matter how irrational they were, I would intentionally flood my mind with the key triggers of my fears. After initially having panic attacks, I eventually realized the consequences would not materialize, despite reliving the obsessions. The linkage between the obsessions and compulsions was faulty. The beauty of ERP is its simplicity and that it, like OCD, does not care about or distinguish among various subtypes. Obsessions are obsessions, and compulsion are compulsions. They all suck.

Harm, Sex, and Religious Obsessions Subtype

Taboos, or behaviors that are considered improper and on the fringe, exist in every society. They are like magnets for OCD because they seem to attract obsessions that lead individuals to seek temporary relief through ritualistic compulsions. Put another way, people with this OCD subtype tend to link particularly strong emotions to taboos. The more offensive the taboo to established social norms, the more OCD is attracted to it. In contemporary society, taboos related to violence, sexuality, and religious orthodoxy are common. The obsessions generated around them can be especially potent.

The overall emotional sense related to this subtype is obsessional.

The overall emotional sense related to this subtype is obsessional. Consider the woman who wants to pray the Hail Mary or Shema in the quiet of her living room. She believes that solitude and concentration are critical for quality prayer. That's reasonable. She begins her routine, only to be distracted by the blue jay loudly singing outside her window or by her spouse doing the dishes in the kitchen. Because she has OCD, she cannot shake the disturbance. Her initial frustration gets 'stuck' in neutral and begins to spiral into something greater—anger. She likely knows her escalating response is not reasonable but feels powerless to stop the cycling of thoughts. On and on…Suddenly, another thought enters her mind. 'Because I was distracted during sacred prayer, maybe I don't want to be close to God. Maybe it's because I'm a child of the Devil.' Later on, perhaps she sees a young boy and has an unwanted sexual thought about him. 'Am I a pedophile?' she asks herself. Why else would she have the thought? She remembers as a teenager having sexual orientation obsessions which caused her distress rather than pleasure when she thought of handsome boys (Clark, 2020). She knew she was homosexual but became anxious when she doubted her orientation. These examples of religious and sexual obsessions can involve cyclic thoughts that, because they are so emotionally charged by the taboos society assigns them, are very difficult to let go. The more one tries to delete these obsessions, the more they seem to stick.

Other obsessive patterns in this subtype can involve violence. The person with this facet of OCD often fears they will carry out the violent images that haunt their thoughts. While research has indicated there is no such linkage,[13] the fear of losing control can overpower rationality, leading to more cycling and snowballing. One fearful thought (*I have this kitchen knife in my hand and could stab someone with it*) can cascade to others (*some bad people have stabbed their spouses…maybe I want to because I'm thinking about it*). Perhaps someone ruminates on opening the cabin door of a plane in flight, continuing to ruminate on it because of the guilt of having the curious thought in the first place. The more the thoughts are connected to taboos (*hurting*

---

13. See Abramowitz (2018) and Clark (2020). Clark describes in greater detail research concerning repugnant obsessions, comorbidities, and cultural tendencies among different religious faiths and national backgrounds.

someone, murder) and loved ones (*partners*), the more emotionally charged they can become. The more charged they are, the harder it is to let go of them. While the obsessions can seem overwhelming, this subtype is not necessarily all about obsessions, or 'PureO.'

While not always apparent, this subtype often involves compulsions to provide short-term relief. The woman praying may say the Shema ten times to 'ensure' at least one counts during a silent moment. Others with thoughts of violating vulnerable others sexually and/or violently may choose to avoid potential triggers. For instance, a person may say to himself, "This documentary about serial killers is not rated 'O' [for my OCD]." The person who fears killing others by opening a cabin door on a plane may choose not to get up out of their seat during a flight. Treatment and therapy should be supervised because they are addressing strong emotions and fears.

Understandably, those being treated with ERP have to appreciate the potentially high levels of distress they may encounter when deliberately exposing themselves to their triggers. Some have found that using counterpunches to these disruptive thought patterns can help change these cycles over time into more positive cognitive habits. For example, *"I could stab my wife with this knife"* could eventually become *"I like cooking with my wife and catching up with her."* It is critical not to ritualize new thought patterns like mantras, lest they become new compulsions. Others have found mindfulness and meditative practices can help empower them to learn to let go and release troublesome obsessions, realizing nothing bad comes from releasing them. I have found a Centering Prayer practice of imagining sitting on a hill looking at the river of my obsessions flowing by is a powerful healing agent. It helps me visualize the reality that the world is not going to implode when I let the obsessions go by.[14]

14. For more information on centering prayer, see Keating (1986/1992/2006) and the website of Contemplative Outreach, which he helped found, at www.contemplativeoutreach.org.

Symmetry, Ordering, and Arranging Subtype

The Symmetry, Ordering, and Arranging (SOA) OCD subtype, unlike the others fueled by fear and doubt, is grounded more in a sense of incompleteness. While outwardly this subtype appears to be perfectionistic, the internal motivation is to correct—to control one's immediate world in order to feel secure.

A person with this subtype is very sensitive to when "something isn't right." The problem with this logic is that the baseline for "normal" is not necessarily rationally defined in his mind. For example, a man cooking a two-egg omelet might have to think through the process of removing the eggs from the carton. With two empty spaces now created in a dozen-sized container, the empty spots can pose a challenge if he believes every container must either be completely full or empty. (Imagine if he was preparing a three-egg omelet for his wife!) He may decide to head off the perceived problem by taking all eggs out of the store containers when he returns from the grocery store and place them into a single, clear container. Suddenly, the potential issue of seeing incomplete containers not being used to their full capacity is temporarily solved with a transparent plastic food storage container. For now. Until that container, too, is near empty in a few days.

> **A person with this subtype is very sensitive to when "something isn't right." The problem with this logic is that the baseline for "normal" is not necessarily rationally defined in his mind.**

In this subtype, thoughts can also cycle. The omelet chef may begin to link the obsessions about incompleteness to other concerns. Eggs can cause salmonella to spread if not handled according to appropriate food safety procedures. Following such procedures, coupled with the lack of symmetry (or sense of balance) in storage container use, could result in great distress. This thinking is based on the premise that there is an all-or-nothing approach to life. I'm right, so you must be wrong. There is very little 'gray' space in this worldview, leaving little room for error for either the person with OCD or his partner. A seemingly harmless obsession about egg storage could blow up into a misperception that, if one doesn't handle the eggs 'properly,' everyone in the family could die of salmonella poisoning. As a result, the married couple may find themselves ritually cleaning the kitchen for several hours every time they take an egg out of a container.

Yet another example of the arranging characteristic may entail this thought pattern: "If I don't order the cash in my wallet properly, the car may crash and kill my entire family." In this case, a sense of responsibility is emotionally—not logically—linked to the manner of ordering bills in a wallet or purse. Of course, what is 'normal' or 'proper' isn't defined by social norms but by one's misperceived experiences and obsessions.

People tend to seek temporary relief from these exhaustive obsessions through many of the cognitive-behavioral approaches already noted. In particular, avoiding the situations that could trigger the obsessions, like not using eggs in your kitchen but buying an omelet instead, is a common tactic. Ordering and arranging items in predictable ways can provide short-term respite, but the obsessions may persist. Mindfulness and ERP training can prove helpful in showing sufferers that they can let go of their obsessions. Additionally, changing cognitive patterns with counterpunches—without, themselves, becoming repetitive mantras—can also empower caregivers not to facilitate their partners' compulsions.

Summary of Subtypes, Effects, and Strategies

The following table summarizes the OCD subtypes in terms of their key effects on relationships and strategies to cope with them.

Table 3.1

Subtype	Effects on Relationships	Coping Strategies
Contamination	**Overall Emotion:** Disgust **Common Obsessions:** •Bodily fluids & excretions •Infecting loved ones •Contaminants **Thought Patterns:** •What if the infection spreads? •What if I infect others? **Common Compulsions:** •Avoidance •Excessive cleaning •Decontamination rituals	**Possible Treatments:** • Exposure & Response Prevention (ERP) with Cognitive Behavioral Therapy (CBT) • Medication • Mindfulness & Meditative Practices as a couple
Doubt, Checking, & Repeating	**Overall Emotion:** Responsibility **Common Obsessions:** • Fear of failure • I'm causing accidents **Thought Patterns:** • What if I didn't lock the door? • What if I forgot my keys? **Common Compulsions:** • Repeatedly check to ensure suitcase is locked • Listen to radio to scan for accidents • Ask for reassurance: e.g., Am I bad? Am I good? Will we be OK?	**Possible Treatments:** • Exposure & Response Prevention (ERP) with CBT • Medication • Mindfulness & Meditative Practices as a couple • Counterpunches (without obsessing over mantras or new rituals) with more positive thinking patterns.

Subtype	Effects on Relationships	Coping Strategies
Harm, Sex, Religious, or Taboo Obsessions	**Overall Emotion:** Obsessive **Common Obsessions:** • Violence & aggression • Sexual • Religious (scrupulosity) **Thought Patterns:** • I could kill any loved one with this knife right now. • What if I opened the plane's door? • If I think these things, it must mean I'm a bad person. **Common Compulsions:** • Relatively subdued but distressing • Ask for reassurance • Thought cycles that easily snowball	**Possible Treatments:** • Exposure & Response Prevention (ERP) with Cognitive Behavioral Therapy (CBT) • Medication • Mindfulness & Meditative Practices as a couple
Symmetry, Ordering, and Arranging (SOA)	**Overall Emotion:** Something isn't right; incompleteness **Common Obsessions:** • Need for certainty • Need for completion of a set • I need balance, in everything **Thought Patterns:** • If I don't order the bills in my wallet 'properly,' the car will crash and kill my family. • I will be responsible **Common Compulsions:** • Precise arranging • Balancing things so they're symmetrical • Hoarding to ensure you'll always have enough to complete a set • Ordering	**Possible Treatments:** • Exposure & Response Prevention (ERP) with CBT • Medication • Mindfulness & Meditative Practices as a couple • Counterpunches (without obsessing over mantras or new rituals)

By identifying the OCD subtypes and their effects on personal relationships, a couple can begin to find ways to treat the obsessions and compulsions with outside assistance and seek ways to combat the negative effects of OCD. Knowing the subtypes can enable a couple to work together to gain a sense of control over daily disruptions and confusing situations.

Learning about OCD subtypes is time well spent because it can provide you tools to survive OCD and thrive in your relationship. It is like arming yourself with knowledge before setting off to battle an enemy—OCD. Sufferers, for instance, can anticipate common thought patterns and obsessions before they cycle into habituated compulsions. Caregivers who understand the type of OCD of their partners can also identify trigger thoughts and behaviors before cycling gets out of control. As a result, couples may become more mindful of indicators and factors that can aggravate or mitigate the OCD in their relationships.

Chapter 4
Do's and Don'ts of Accommodating OCD in the Marriage

Accommodating OCD

Being a spouse of someone with OCD can make everyday life challenging. Partners work together in a typical marriage to decide who will perform various tasks on a daily basis. OCD adds another layer of tasks that only one partner can manage. This can result in what seems like two times the work as additional responsibilities are added because the partner with OCD has fears related to the disorder. These additional responsibilities can include tasks that must be done because of the other's day to day challenges. Going out as a couple into social situations can add another complex layer as the partner tries to nullify the obsessions and compulsions as much as possible. There is a wide range of emotions that are experienced by a partner of someone who has OCD on any given day.

Accommodations are ways we help our loved ones while helping the relationship function as well as possible. By sitting in one place and listening to David's daily brief about the events of his day, I was adjusting my life to help manage his fear that he would forget to tell me something, meaning he wouldn't tell me everything, meaning there was imperfect communication, which (because communication is essential to all marriages, so they say) ultimately would lead to the demise of our marriage. Yes, it was that complicated. I realize now that by making accommodations to lessen David's fears, I was actually feeding into his OCD and allowing the hungry animal that is OCD to grow. I was adjusting my routine to "help" David, resulting in negative consequences for the two of us. My accommodations were ultimately making the daily briefings longer and longer—lasting up to an hour at a time.

Fabrizio Didonna (2020), a professor in the Institute for Lifelong Learning of the University of Barcelona in Spain, offers the following guidelines for family members and partners of what to do and what not to do to help people who have OCD.[15] Some of these guidelines include:

1. Never give reassurances that feed into a compulsion. When your partner asks for reassurance, you can remind them that it will only provide temporary relief.

2. Never help partners with their rituals. Formalizing compulsions by helping with the rituals can normalize them and reinforce obsessive fears.

3. Don't limit your life's experiences because of your loved one's OCD problems. It's OK to seek help for yourself.

4. Never blame your partner for his or her OCD problems. Didonna (2020) reminds us that "OCD is not his or her fault. Your loved one is a victim of the disorder and just needs help" (p. 187).

5. Don't get discouraged by setbacks. Improvement will come before and after them. Lapses are typical during stressful times.

---

15. See Didonna (2020) p. 183 for the complete list. Items 6–11 are direct quotes.

6. Give your loved one messages of trust and confidence in his or her recovery.

7. Help your loved one become independent.

8. Recognize, encourage, and praise your loved one for small improvements.

9. Believe in your loved one's ability to manage and overcome OCD.

10. Use humor.

11. Try to recognize signs that signal when your loved one's OCD might be active.

Keeping these guidelines in mind can help set healthy boundaries in a relationship with OCD. Unbeknownst to me, I was participating in David's rituals to help him avoid his anxiety of leaving even the smallest detail out. What I thought was helping his anxiety was making it easier for David to perform his rituals without any pushback. This was not the desired result.

Another way I found myself accommodating David's OCD was by avoiding certain movies and daily situations where he might see an attractive woman and worry excessively about running off with her or questioning why he married me when there were so many beautiful women in the world. It was overwhelming to go to concerts or travel or shop and have to hear about his obsessions about the way other women looked or dressed. By avoiding certain situations, I found myself in a place where I was afraid to go in public with him for fear that I would have to hear how good-looking other women were. The cycle was perpetual. I would even entertain these thoughts when we weren't in these situations or around other people. Even though I knew these were irrational thoughts and comments that he was making, I couldn't find any accommodation that would stop or lessen the behavior. The result was that we both felt awful.

Changing routines, schedules, and plans are accommodations for a person with OCD. David has certain routines he has to do before going for a ride in the car—no matter the distance of the drive. It can be a trip to the grocery store or a long road trip to another state—we have to adjust our start time to go anywhere to add the time it takes for David to finish his many rituals and routines. We can be running late to go somewhere, but he still has to finish his rituals. It's as if his sense of time is not affected by his perceived need to perform these compulsions.

As Abramowitz (2021) writes, accommodations can be protective, but ineffective. None of us wants to see the person we love and care about anxious and hurting. We want to protect them as much as possible, resulting in the many accommodations we provide. Accommodations can ultimately give energy to the OCD, as was the case of David's daily briefings. Sitting and listening to his one-sided brief added to the time that I was his "captive audience." Instead of lessening his anxiety about the brief, David's OCD took full advantage of the opportunity and got stronger as he navigated throughout his day, writing the smallest detail down to share with me at the end of the day.

Chapter 5
Our Levels of Awareness: How did we know?

The stories we shared earlier describe our experience as a married couple living with OCD and its many challenges. Emotionally, these experiences have spanned a broad spectrum, from despair to loneliness, to anger, and even hope. These emotions seemed to be tied to our awareness of OCD and its impacts on our married life. For example, I would feel angry at myself for forcing my wife to stand and listen to my daily brief written in miniscule, precise handwriting while knowing that it was not normal. On the other hand, Michaela and I now sometimes laugh together when we talk about Herb (the name we have given the OCD that wants to act as a third member of our marriage) and how much we dislike him. As we have become more aware of how OCD affects us, we have become more empowered to do something about it. It's been our choice all along.

Our Three Primary Levels of Awareness

Acknowledging a third person, admission of a need to heal, and seeking professional treatment. This increased awareness over time has enabled us to make informed decisions about the disorder. While not every couple may have equal degrees of insight into their disorder, we hope our story can help provide some context of coping with OCD in married life.

1 A Third Person in the Marriage

My mother tended to exaggerate the pronunciation of certain words. One of our favorites was how she said "h-erbs," with a hard "h" sound, that were in her cooking garden. She spoke of them with some respect because they were key ingredients in many of her gourmet meals. When we adopted "Herb" to name our OCD, it was with similar respect and some humor. We wanted to acknowledge the OCD as our own but not take it so seriously that we would always fear it.

Today, we still acknowledge Herb's presence when I obsessively cycle with uncommanded thoughts or compulsively brief Michaela. It gives my wife an opportunity to vent her frustrations not on her partner but on the source of her pain. Yet, this third person also reminds us that this is our disorder to handle—we cannot blame the world or anyone else in it. Herb is a powerful concoction that enables us to take control and responsibility for our responses to OCD and to each other. No wonder Michaela periodically says in response to my compulsive comments and rigid behavior: "I hate Herb!" I know exactly what she means because I feel the same way. It's OK to hate the OCD—we have learned to deal with it in a different way. Herb cannot be reasoned with or given rationales. Joking about Herb allows us to laugh about things and portray things that I do in a more lighthearted way, lessening the intensity of the situation and grounding us in the reason why I feel compelled to do things a certain way.

2 **Courage to Admit the Need for Healing**

Before we could name the root cause of many of our marital problems, we had to decide to seek professional help. Not every clinician has the tools to diagnose or treat OCD and related disorders. We encountered well-intended clinicians who had many certificates, but none who were trained to identify characteristics of OCD. Still, we persevered. Eventually, we were lucky to find a clinician who listened, who had experience in addressing OCD, and who told us plainly what we were facing.

As a male in the military, I lived in a culture in which showing your best face was critical to how others judged you and considered you for promotion. Putting on masks to cover OCD was as routine as putting on uniforms. And we both wore masks as husband and wife—sometimes with each other. We didn't want others to know about the OCD and went to painstaking lengths to hide my OCD when we were around others. The OCD in our marriage was like a pot of boiling water with a lid that was preventing contents from spilling over. This disciplined use of masks to present our false selves to the world hurt our openness to each other, causing a division that made it easier to fight over insignificant issues. For me, my inflexible routines became so important that I was physically rigid in my interactions with others. This inflexibility made me lack trust in my partner that she had my best interests at heart, that telling me I was cycling wasn't an affront to my manhood but a fact of which I needed to be aware.

3 **Diagnosis and Treatment for Both of You**

After the initial relief of diagnosis previously described, we soon realized this is a family disease that demands commitment from all family members. For us, it meant coordinating schedules to meet the therapist regularly, patience with systemic medications that can take a month or so to exhibit therapeutic effects, and humility to admit shortcomings. I not only had to trust my life partner when she pointed out my cycling obsessions, but I also had to convince myself that I could admit my weaknesses. This was one of the hardest things I have ever had to do, and the struggle continues. We have found solace in couple's prayer,[16] traveling to new destinations, meditation, and mindful walking—activities that allow us to be intentionally present to one another. Participating in activities as a couple has been critical for us in order to be more present to each other. Paul notes that "…my power is at its best in weakness…. For it is when I am weak that I am strong" (2 Cor. 12:9-10, *Jerusalem Bible*). In other words, it's OK to ask for help, especially if something as important as your marriage is at stake. Rather than judgment, you may find that others—including yourselves—will offer you both love and support.

Ah, a Checklist!

No one seems to like checklists more than obsessive checkers. Soon after my diagnosis, I realized how much checklists were integral to myriad facets of my life. Checklists provided me, a pilot, guided steps to turn on and shut down aircraft safely. As a program planner, action lists in regulations helped ensure I did not overlook a critical aspect of a complex problem. As a husband with OCD, I crafted daily lists of items to convey to Michaela, whether she wanted them or not. I had to tell her about what I did, uncertainties, doubts, actions, decisions—all based on the fear that omitting information was tantamount to sabotaging our communication and trust, thereby ruining the marriage bond. While briefing her was a very ingrained compulsion, the list itself became a symbol of our OCD challenges.

Not much later, the psychiatrist who initiated my medications reverentially commented on my briefing compulsion: "Ah, …a liiist!" It came across to us as something very funny because he seemed to

16. Michaela here—This has been very hard for me because I have had to differentiate between David's compulsive, scrupulous praying and authentic couples prayer. It has taken us 20 years to get to that level of trust. The lesson? Healing together does not happen overnight. It takes patience and persistence.

regard it as a key indicator of my diagnosis. Nonetheless, Michaela and I periodically say that universal truth to one another as a light reminder of where we have been and how far we have journeyed.

Another way I have used lists compulsively is using them as tools to record milestones and achievements. Writing things down in a precise manner, regardless of format, seems to be a way to address the fear of forgetting lessons learned, promises made, or even groceries to purchase. The fear, for me, was very real, because there was a direct line from a decline in communication to divorce. I couldn't see it any other way. I even created a certificate declaring I had shared all of my pre-marital experiences with my young wife to ensure no lie existed between us. I also created a list of renewed marriage vows (Figure 10.3). Then, before Thanksgiving in the eighth year of our marriage, I felt an impulse to craft a list of life lessons as shown in Figure 5.1 (page 44). Here, the fear was losing hard-earned wisdom (mostly through study and observing several speakers) to become a better person. The irrational linkage was that losing such wisdom meant I was too lazy to keep it and too unworthy to improve. OCD has infected many, if not most, aspects of our lives. Being mindful of these issues better prepared us for treatment.

Figure 5.1

David's List of Life Lessons

- It ain't as bad as you think. It will look better in the morning.
- Get mad, then get over it.
- Avoid having your ego so close to your position that, when your position falls, your ego goes with it.
- It can be done!
- Positive attitude and leadership are force multipliers.
- Be careful what you choose; you may get it.
- Don't let adverse facts stand in the way of good decisions.
- You can't make someone else's decisions. You shouldn't let someone else make yours.
- Check small things. Pay attention to detail.
- Share credit.
- Remain calm.
- Be kind, and treat others with respect—regardless of rank or position (Golden Rule).
- Have a vision. Be demanding.
- Change to improve things that you understand, not for change's sake.
- Don't take counsel of your fears or naysayers/critics.
- Life is simple; it's our decisions that make it complicated.
- Accept the consequences, and don't offer excuses.
- Know when to sit down and shut up.

- Listen to others (especially subordinates); be inclusive and don't interrupt.
- Be brief: in speech, writing, and presenting.
- Exercise creativity: draw, write poems, read, practice another language, hike.
- Don't judge others.
- Smile, and say what you mean.
- Each day, ask how you can be more helpful to all beings. Make things better where you can.
- Each day, balance yourself physically, mentally, & spiritually.
- Let people do their jobs; provide them the tools to do their jobs, and specify your expectations of them.
- Be a "we"—not an "I"— leader.
- Don't walk by a problem.
- Never criticize a predecessor.
- It's better to wear out than to rust out.
- A shot not taken is a shot missed.
- Be a critical thinker.
- Know your priorities: God, family, friends, you.
- Give God permission to enter your life; be thankful.
- Be quick to listen and think fast. Talk slower.
- Replace anger, bitterness, and impatience with compassion, love, and patience.

Dated: 19 November 2003
Sources: GEN Eberhardt, GEN (Ret.) Colin Powell, and personal experiences

Chapter 6
Mindfulness and Treatment

Mindfulness has been a topic of discussion in clinical and public areas over the past few years. Since OCD can distress any marital partnership, anything that can offer ways to reduce the anxiety and stress that accompany OCD is worthy of consideration. In this section, we'll examine what mindfulness is, the disruptive nature of OCD, mindfulness as a coping mechanism for couples, and partner support.

What is Mindfulness?

Mindfulness is a state of self-awareness that allows us to monitor our thoughts and observe the continuous flow of cognitive processes.[17] In a way, it consists of thinking about thinking—or metacognition. By becoming more aware of what we think at various times, we can begin to see through raw emotions and identify 'real' information upon which we can develop more accurate perceptions of reality. Beyond metacognition, mindfulness involves recognition of the various filters we use to make sense of daily life. Mindfulness,

---

17. See Beverley, 2004/2008, p. 147 and Didonna, 2020, Chapters 2 & 5.

in this sense, involves looking at something just as it is – without bias or preconception. If we adopted the mind of a child looking at something for the very first time, we would be in a mindful state.

How OCD Disrupts Peace in Partnerships

OCD is a disorder, as previously discussed, because it can disrupt peace in relationships—whether with self, friends, or partners. By highlighting a person's egotistic obsessions, the disorder can delay growth in compassion for and communication with a partner. Undesired intrusive thoughts, grounded in unfounded perceptions of reality, can lead to an erosion of trust and empathy in any relationship (Clark & O'Connor, 2005). OCD tends to amplify doubts we can get when learning from our experiences through our senses, resulting in a false narrative about ourselves and our relationships.[18] Abramowitz (2021) describes OCD as a con artist, making a couple believe they can solve a simple problem that, the more they 'fix' it, becomes increasingly unsolvable and emotionally charged. As a result, the relationship becomes distressed over time, often without any relief.

How Mindfulness Can Help Couples Cope with OCD

Mindfulness can help identify misperceptions and thereby empower us to retell our narratives grounded in our senses rather than imaginary doubts. Meditative practices can help develop and preserve mindfulness by linking physical and mental relaxation. Mindfulness can help reduce OCD symptoms and nurture a sense of peace and wellbeing.[19]

Couples can use these mindful practices to change the rules and gain the upper hand over the OCD 'con artist.' By physically and mentally controlling one's personal space through mindful awareness, one can begin to feel more confident—not only about

---

18. For more information on OCD and mindfulness, see Abramowitz (2021, Chapters 2-3), Clark & O'Connor (2005, Chapter 6), and Didonna (2020, Chapters 3 & 6-7).
19. See Didonna (2020, p. 168).

himself but also his partner. For example, by placing oneself in an upright and relaxed meditative pose, conducting breathing exercises in a space that normally triggers obsessive thoughts (for example, germs in a bathroom), he can begin to equate that space with centeredness and relaxation. Put another way, mindfulness activities can help us correct misperceptions of our own realities through open mindedness and cultivated compassion.

Helping Partners Support their Loved Ones

Mindfulness and other constructive activities don't just help patients; they can also support loved ones who care for their partners. The same open-minded approach that can help correct faulty logic patterns in patients can also help caregivers recognize how they may be accommodating them. The wife of the man triggered by germophobic obsessions can meditate with him in the bathroom— the scene of the con. While he may more clearly identify his misplaced fears, she may discern how helping him ritually clean the bathroom only facilitates his compulsions. At the same time, the act of doing the activity together exhibits mutual support and encouragement along the long road of healing. Other activities that promote mindfulness, listed on the following pages, may likewise enable couples to better cope with OCD.

Mindfulness Activities That Can Help Couples Better Cope with OCD

- **Journaling** – Write about something for which you are grateful every day. Be specific and think about how something, or someone, makes your life better. Being grateful for the 'littlest' things can help us appreciate the truly important people in our lives.

- **Sitting Meditation** – Find a quiet space where you won't be disturbed. Sit upright and concentrate on your posture and breathing—nothing else. Relax. When thoughts or images intrude, let them pass by and continue to focus on breathing. Set your timer for 10–20 minutes and increase the time as your schedule allows.

- **Breathing Exercises** – While sitting, walking, or doing daily chores, become aware of your breathing. In and out. In and out. In and out. If you desire, choose a concise, meaningful quote from a sacred text or author to say while you inhale and exhale. For example, "God is [inhale]…love [exhale]" or "Be love [inhale]…to others [exhale]." Avoid saying the words or phrases compulsively as mantras. Just say them as you feel the need to center.

- **Walking Meditation** – Choose a quiet area where you can walk comfortably and safely, undisturbed for 15-20 minutes. Maintain a good posture and let yourself be quiet inside so you can listen to your surroundings. Tune in to the environment. Slowly, deliberately step forward. Let thoughts and images pass by in no particular order. Pray, think of a sacred image, or ponder a certain saying. Center your thoughts and feelings. People with OCD may find this active meditative practice helpful if sitting still for extended periods is challenging (Didonna, 2020).

- **Labyrinth Walk** – This meditative practice is similar to walking meditation, and it adds the labyrinth as a metaphor for life's journey. The labyrinth is a physical structure that allows a person to enter a safe space where they encounter sacredness and then return to themselves in time and space. It is conducive to prayer because it links physical sense making to internal peace. The combination of movement and meditation can be a powerful response to distressing obsessive-compulsive cycles.

- **Centering Prayer** – Grounded in classic monasticism, this practice of contemplative prayer can help someone reconnect to their true selves—as opposed to their obsessive egos. Like sitting meditation, find a quiet space where you won't be disturbed for at least 20 minutes. Breathe. The practice is simple but requires practice of 4 basic guidelines: 1) Choose a sacred word or phrase that symbolizes your intent to consent to God's presence and action within, 2) sit quietly with closed eyes and peacefully introduce your sacred word/phrase, 3) say the sacred word/phrase when thoughts or images disturb you, and 4) when the alarm sounds, remain quiet for a few minutes. Contemplative Outreach has an application and a helpful website with many useful resources.

- **Forest Bathing** – If you like nature and find it easy to find your center there, this meditative practice may be effective. The purpose is to slow down and become immersed in the natural environment by taking in surroundings using all of the senses. The practice of forest bathing can help boost immunity and restore one's mood and can help reduce stress and worry by helping a person to think more clearly.

- **Physical Exercise** – This elevates endorphin levels – Find an activity or hobby that is healthy and focuses your attention away from obsessive-compulsive cycles. For many, cardiovascular exercises such as running, hiking, biking, or swimming can improve fitness and stimulate an overall sense of wellbeing.

- **Yoga** – This is another mind-body practice developed over centuries. It can effectively link meditative practice to physical well-being and breathing.

- **Tai Chi** – This is an ancient Chinese mind-body practice that allows someone to focus on their body rather than intrusive thoughts and obsessive-compulsive cycles. It is another mindful option available to OCD survivors, both sufferers and their caregivers.

Chapter 7
Examples from Our Experiences

The following stories are OCD-related challenges we have faced in our relationship. They are examples of situations in our marriage in which we have grown together in confronting the disorder and its disruptions. We have set up each experience by giving a short example of a challenge that we have faced, the research behind what was happening at the time, and tips that we have found helpful and healing in our marriage. We selected these particular stories because they are moments that have helped us to face the fact that OCD will always be present in our lives and they are ways we have dealt creatively with OCD in our marriage. While they may not all apply to your situation, you may be able to glean some bits of wisdom that you can use to improve your own relationship. We hope they resonate with you.

EXPERIENCE #1:
Naming the Third Member of our Marriage

Example

Herb lurks in the background of our marriage. He's an archetype, more than an imaginary figment, but also not a delusion. His name allows us to label and target our opponent, thereby making us stronger in our alliance. We often joke that we "left Herb back home" during vacations that are going well. Of course, we'll remark, "I hate, Herb!" when the obsessions begin to take over pleasant conversation during our couple time.

What the Research Says

People can effectively change their behavior and thought patterns by how they conceptualize OCD.[21] Schwartz and Beyette (1996/2016) describe how the neuroplasticity of the brain enables individuals and couples to change the brain functions of OCD sufferers. This implies that changing the environment by how we perceive OCD can affect how we respond to it. When we respond to OCD flare ups by light heartedly labeling it by a name, we normalize the disorder's effects— we recognize for what it is and nothing more. In this manner, we refuse to give it more credit than it's due.

Tips for Healing

If you're married, you have already worked through some difficult and complex problems together. The key is to continue to communicate with each other and remember that you're in it as a team. Objectifying the disorder by calling it a playful name has enabled us to communicate and recognize OCD's presence without emotionally draining our relationship.

---

21. See Culkin, 2016 and 2019. See also Schwartz & Beyette, 1996/2016.

"Why me? He's broken!"

Example

Yep, Michaela said I was "broken" when describing my obsessive thoughts to our therapist after our diagnosis. At first, it was difficult to accept, but its truth washed away some of the protective veneer with which I have lacquered my personality over decades of surviving with OCD.

What the Research Says

Recognizing there is a problem is a very difficult step for many couples. Since many sufferers refuse to acknowledge the need for help even while symptoms worsen, "early diagnosis and effective treatment of OCD are essential to curtail its multidimensional" characteristics (Koen & Stein, 2015, p. 623). While OCD may entail some genetic roots, biochemical imbalances, and environmental triggers, identifying them with each other and a trained therapist can be very powerful in developing a holistic understanding of the disorder in the marriage and what can be done about it.[22] Furthermore, there is no compelling evidence that OCD sufferers' obsessive thoughts cause or contribute to the catastrophic, destructive behaviors they fear. [23]

Tips for Healing

Discussing the issues and their possible causes are a significant part of healing in any marriage. This is particularly true for marriages with OCD. Setting aside a time to report to each other can promote mutual accountability. Sometimes, when we cannot attend a session together, we find it helpful for the absent partner to write the therapist a note. The note can be as simple or as deep as necessary. For example, "No changes since last session" or "In the past few weeks, David has

---

22. APA, 2013a; Koen & Stein, 2015; Minelli & Maffioletti, 2014; Schwartz & Beyette, 1996/2016.
23. Baer, 2002; Schwartz & Beyette, 1996/2016.

reverted several times: first..., second..., etc." Providing therapists with more data, not necessarily emotion, can be extremely helpful in therapeutic decision making. When partners have separate therapy sessions, a letter to the therapist can complement the picture painted for the clinician.

EXPERIENCE #3:
"Oh, I have OCD too!"

Example

One day, I went to a doctor, not my primary care provider, for an emergency refill of my OCD medication. It was a stressful time, and I was very grateful I had the opportunity to get help before my prescription was depleted. An older but robust man, he commented when writing the slip that he had OCD too. He proceeded to describe his perfectionist tendencies and how they helped him to get through medical school, accomplish his life goals, and be successful. I appreciated his positive outlook, but I couldn't deny feeling that his arbitrary review somehow diminished Michaela and my negative experiences with the disorder. To compound my frustration, I felt that I couldn't judge his self-report because I may not have known his complete story and was not qualified to make a diagnosis. Then, I got a little angry inside, realizing that he had placed his traits—regardless of severity—above our reality.

What the Research Says

Many who claim they have OCD merely have traits. "The intense pain and suffering caused by OCD is not something a sufferer with real OCD would ever speak of in a glib or casual manner" (Schwartz & Beyette, 1996/2016, p. xxiv). In other words, OCD entails a cost in terms of time (often several hours a day), guilt, and functionality (sometimes debilitating) that goes beyond normally acceptable behavior.[24]

---

24. APA, 2013a; Baer, 2002.

Tips for Healing

People may say they have OCD in passing without considering your own experiences. Focus less on what they claim and more on addressing the challenges that face your partner and you. Taking time as a married couple to share experiences, feelings, doubts, and conflicts about OCD is a powerful and effective tool. Opening our hearts and minds to the possible paths of meaning can promote habits of communication that remind us that we are there for one another. We are not alone, especially in marriage.

EXPERIENCE #4:
Uncommanded Thoughts and Brief Lists

Example

Uncommanded thoughts are probably one of the hardest things for me to explain. I can be anywhere, whether in public or private, and have a thought that makes no sense but triggers an intense emotion. It can be whether or not I want to run off with another woman or if I want to hurt someone I love. Social taboos are common fodder. While everyone has crazy thoughts at times, these thoughts are different. They don't go away. In fact, the more I try to expunge them, the more 'sticky' they seem to become, adhering to the doubts and fears coating my brain. As a result, I may ruminate for hours on the same thought or snowball into a cascade of unlikely and implausible paradoxes. This cycling can be quite exhausting.

My daily briefs to Michaela, especially during the early years of our marriage before I was treated, exemplify the insidious effects of obsessive thoughts in relationships. Any doubts or uncertainties I would entertain during the day would make my "list." The list would take many different forms: e-mails, texts, phone calls, or scraps of paper. I would rigidly read the comments to her. This compulsion would temporarily assuage my fear that if I didn't tell her everything, it would mean our communication was broken, and broken communication inevitably led to divorce. I was unable to see the irrational logic trail because I was overcome by the fear of uncertainty. This is one of my stronger compulsions because I still do it—albeit with less frequency, severity, and rigidity.

What the Research Says

OCD can negatively impact relationships: "…some individuals with OCD try to impose rules and prohibitions on family members because of their disorder (for example, no one in the family can have visitors to the house for fear of contamination), and this can lead to family dysfunction."[25] The caudate nucleus acts as the brain's filter that, when malfunctioning, can create imbalance and result in inefficient filtering of thoughts, urges, and fears.[26]

Tips for Healing

Seek someone you, as a couple, can trust outside of the marriage with whom you can share your OCD story. Sharing your experiences with neutral persons, as we do with our therapist, can help you identify irrational obsessions and realize that their resultant obsessions do not really address them. Furthermore, inserting humor in the give-and-take of marital relationships can alleviate some friction points. For example, my wife will often try to trick me and grab my brief list mentioned previously. She has also been known to hide my list and play a sort of "hotter and colder" game to find it. This playful attitude helps us both vent the frustration of dealing with this ritual after twenty plus years while downplaying its importance.

25. APA, 2013a, p. 241; see also Hyman & Pedrick, 1999.
26. Schwartz & Beyette, 1996/2016.

EXPERIENCE #5:
Storytelling and Humor

Example

Our personal stories of OCD thus far in this book describe key themes in our relationship. Each of our stories informs the bigger story of our relationship. While each story has a beginning, middle, and end, each also addresses very different facets of the relationship. For example, David's stories tend to deeply reflect upon his thoughts and ruminations that lead to exhausting compulsions. Michaela's perspective, however, tends to focus on the emotional responses to the irrational behaviors and surviving long-term caregiving. Over the years, we have continued to write our story and have thereby gained more empowerment. The storyline may be OCD, but we are the authors.

What the Research Says

Literary techniques can help OCD sufferers communicate their symptoms to their partners, themselves, and their therapists.

Storytelling and metaphor use are often the best ways to present subtle and confusing ideas in a succinct and concrete way. In fact, they are wonderful ways to go beyond merely describing something or even explaining it. Narratives serve to illustrate not just an idea, but the very foundation of an idea. (Weg, 2011, p. 4)

Put another way, we define ourselves through stories. Coupling stories and humor can be a powerful combination. Developing one's humor and practicing it with loved ones can promote psychological and immunological benefits while maintaining perspective on what's important.[27] Over time, narrating the personal struggle with the disorder to trusted others can record transformational progress and enhance the self-agency of sufferers.[28]

---

27. Brown, 2001.
28. Baer, 2002; Culkin, 2016, 2019; Schmid, 2010; Schwartz & Beyette, 1996/2016; Weg, 2011.

Tips for Healing

Co-writing your OCD story with your partner can be a powerful healing experience. Tell your story (to each other, your journal, or support group), listen to and reflect upon that story, and retell it as a couple in a way you want to recall it. Preparing to tell it can take years due to your particular level of awareness, willingness to seek help, desire to work together, and ability to trust your partner's critiques. For example, it took over twenty years before Michaela felt comfortable enough to go on a religious retreat with me—trauma from public humiliations in which I would spontaneously place my hand on her head so my prayers would be 'perfect.' Collaborating with your spouse is critical in the healing process because you both are affected by the disorder.

EXPERIENCE #6:
What if this is as good as it gets?

Example

Nothing is more entertaining than watching an OCD person struggle with the decision to watch a movie or video that vividly portrays the disorder or its personal triggers. Michaela and I actively discuss whether particular movies are "Rated D" or not. The "D" stands for David. Our evaluation criteria normally entail how close scenes or themes will likely replicate my triggers for obsessive-compulsive cycles. For example, when I was a teenager and living alone with my Mom, I watched a suspense-thriller in which, although not graphic, a lonely mother got a little too close to her son as a confidant. I saw many parallels in my own life and feared I would end up like the boy, breaking up the family and causing public distress. My recurring thoughts snowballed to the point that it was hard for me to distinguish between them and reality. The obsession sparked by the movie bothered me for years. I knew being consumed by my thoughts was not a normal preoccupation, but I couldn't force them out of my mind—

even though nothing similar ever happened with my mother. In fact, the harder I tried to flush the imagery, the more it flared. I didn't know what to do other than journal about it. I later analyzed these journal entries to make sense of them for my dissertation.[29] Looking back now, the obsession is a memory without an emotional tag but serves as a lasting reminder of the pain I've experienced. Having looked at my journals, I could objectively identify these cycles as purely OCD. I have learned that reflecting on past obsessive cycles can help provide me perspective on cycles I continue to endure in our marriage.

What the Research Says

Visual triggers for obsessive-compulsive cycles can be very vivid and disturbing. It can leave one questioning if cycling will ever get better. In the Academy-Award winning *As Good as It Gets* (Brooks, 1997) the protagonist, a grouchy middle-aged man with OCD, asks, "Is this as good as it gets?" after completing his compulsive bathroom ablutions for over an hour while his dinner date waits. My cleaning compulsions aren't as severe as his, but I can relate to the mental turmoil and time drain caused by cycling, cycling, cycling and then realizing how irrational it all is.

Tips for Healing

Develop an action plan in which both of you play a key role. On the left half of a paper, write down a list of triggers you might have watching a movie or reading a book—anything that will start an obsessive-compulsive cycle. For example, possible triggers could include (but not be limited to) a murder scene, a documentary on serial killers, a show on real crime, or any media about social taboos. Taking cues from ongoing exposure response prevention (ERP) therapy, consider how those triggers affect your senses and are rooted in your fears. Write those senses and fears down in the center of the page. On the right margin, identify specific activities or behaviors that you can choose to avoid or practice ERP. For example, a draft plan for our movie/online

29. Culkin, 2016, 2019.

habits may look like Table 7.1. This table could help serve as a guide for types of movies to avoid (horror films and real crime for me) or to use, with guidance of your therapist, for ERP. This worksheet could also inform a more detailed action plan as in Table 14.1 or the template in Chapter 17 (Table 17.1).

Table 7.1
Coping with Triggers in Visual Media

Triggers	Senses and Fears Affected	Activities / Behaviors
Excessive blood and gore	• Visual • That I like it too much and would do something like this because I'm physically capable. In other words, "What's stopping me?"	• Avoid horror movies • Avoid true crime films involving excessive violence • Read horror classics (e.g., *Dracula, Frankenstein*) because they've been analyzed over time and are familiar stories
Social taboos	• Visual • That I would do any of these behaviors—because I physically can—and thus be socially destroyed and end our marriage	• Avoid movies that exaggerate stereotypes and violence at the expense of vulnerable others • Read stories of real people who have overcome these behaviors

Triggers	Senses and Fears Affected	Activities / Behaviors
Sympathy for psychopathic characters	• Visual • That I would become like them because I possibly think like them	• Avoid movies that victimize the ostracized and vulnerable for the purposes of hate and division • Read stories of real people who have survived true hate and violence against all odds—Harriet Tubman, Holocaust survivors, the falsely incarcerated, etc.
Murder of wife	• Visual, touch • That I would do these things because I sometimes obsess about them	• Avoid movies or stories that justify this behavior • Read stories of real people who have avoided or survived domestic violence • Support local domestic violence advocacy groups
Real crime: such as serial murder	• Visual • That I could perpetrate these behaviors	• Avoid movies or stories that justify this behavior • Read stories of real people who have survived/witnessed this behavior and have overcome

---

Experience #7:
Death Therapy!

Example

There's a scene in the comedy *What About Bob?* (Oz, 1991) in which a man afflicted with severe OCD drives his therapist to the brink of his patience. The patient Bob, played by Bill Murray, is very knowledgeable about the disorder and can quote his doctor's popular self-help book at will. Reaching the limit of his patience with his stalking patient, the therapist decides to provide Bob a final session. It involves strapping a bomb to Bob's chest with a trigger that will detonate if he escapes his confinement. (Remember, it's a comedy....) Bob chooses to see this horrifying scenario as a great opportunity to learn to face his fears. He thinks this 'death therapy' is brilliant! His challenges became his opportunity. Bob ends up writing his own book called Death Therapy and becomes a therapist in his own right. At the conclusion of the movie, he still has OCD, but learns to live with it. We quote many lines from this movie quite often in our marriage to bring comedy to the serious situations we can face. Humor can be a helpful tool to lighten the gravity of living with OCD.

What the Research Says

While the therapist in the movie goes to extremes for comedic purposes, effective therapy can help couples safely handle issues unique to their relationships. OCD therapy should target specific symptoms over a period of time in order to promote effective cognitive-behavioral transformation.[30] ERP, medication, stress management, and other therapies can be tailored to the individual needs of OCD sufferers and their families.

---

30. Strauss et al., 2018; Tang et al., 2018.

Tips for Healing

Develop an action plan that lists your particular obsession-compulsion cycles. Select the least emotionally-charged cycle on which to practice. Conduct a mental experiment in which you follow the cycle as far as you can. You may feel anxious, but that's OK. You're in a safe place. Write a quick reflection in your journal about how you felt afterwards. Did you survive without doing the related compulsion? What would your spouse say if they were in your head while writing this reflection?

For example, I am more of an obsessive checker. My mental experiment could entail forgetting my briefcase or losing papers I need for a meeting. I get to work, tell my boss, and—enraged—he fires me. I have no income and lose my wife because I can't support her. All because I failed to check that my case was in my car when I left for work. When I reflect upon this exercise, I realize that the extraordinary logic trail is quite preposterous and doesn't reflect my inner turmoil. There is significant cognitive dissonance, and I know it. I could then share this disconnect with my spouse and/or therapist to elicit specific feedback.

Michaela and I have gotten to a point where we will participate in this exercise out loud and together. We ask each other what would be the worst outcome if I responded to a certain trigger. Then, with each response, we ask the same question again: "What would be the worst thing to happen if you followed through with this?" Inevitably, it becomes clear we've reached an imaginary ending that would never realistically happen. In a strange way, it reaffirms the irrationality of the contrived obsessive-compulsive cycle.

Experience #8:
Sex and Violence

Example

Sexual and violent obsessive thoughts tend to go together. While I lived with my mother, I sometimes feared I could be an Oedipus, especially when I was studying Greek mythology in school. When combing my dog, I wondered if I could strangle this innocent, small, vulnerable creature that trusted me implicitly. When I started living with my wife, I began to fear I could stab her or push her down the stairs without anyone noticing. When I was in college, I feared I had a crush on another male student and didn't know how to deal with it given the social norms of the institution. I would often question my sexual identity and orientation, all the while realizing I was heterosexual. This abyss between my thoughts and actions resulted in cognitive dissonance. The more I thought about these morbid obsessions fueled by my fears, the more emotionally lurid they became, intensifying the uncertainty and doubt I felt. None of the actions noted above occurred or were fulfilled, but the charged thoughts were disturbingly real.

What the Research Says

Obsessions are really impulsive thoughts that emotionally stick. They take up a lot of time and tend to surface the more we try to repress them. And the uninvited thoughts can stubbornly attach to any social taboo or controversial issue at any inappropriate time. OCD can manifest as uncommanded thoughts related to sexual orientation and can possibly have some linkage to people who exhibit sexually addictive behavior. Even though the obsessions are separate from sexual addictive behaviors, they both can be treated. When obsessions are more difficult to expunge, it becomes harder for a person to believe they are sane, socially acceptable, or even a good person.[31]

31. Obsessions tend to occur at the most inopportune moments in our lives (APA, 2013a). These intrusive thoughts tend to attach to social lines related to sexuality and violence (Baer, 2002; Hyman & Pedrick, 1999; Samantaray et al., 2019). Other specific areas of these cognitions include sexual orientation (Coimbra-Gomes & Motschenbacher, 2019), addictions, and self-destructive behavior (Baldacchino & Baldacchino, 2016).

Tips for Healing

Develop an action plan that challenges your thinking patterns. Listing your irrational fears and connecting them to realistic counternarratives can help you adjust your cognitive habits over time and practice (Hyman & Pedrick, 1999). You could then implement these counterpunches in the strategy of your action plan you created in Table 1. Remember that these counterpunches are not, themselves, things to memorize and repeat compulsively. (The last thing you want is another compulsion!) Entering these thoughts in your journal and meditating on them could also foster cognitive transformation by recognizing how fear feeds doubt. See Table 17.2.

Table 7.2
Counterpunching Irrational Cognitive Habits on Sex and Violence

Irrational Cognitive Fear	Realistic Counterpunch
I must be evil to think I find that woman attractive.	*Nothing bad will happen if I think about this. The strength of my relationship with my wife is stronger than the temptation.*
I must turn the car around to make sure I didn't run over that person.	*If I turn around, I will just facilitate my obsession.*
I must clean this many times to be sure I won't get infected and/or die or hurt someone else.	*I can clean it once and be OK.*
I will become a psychopath if I keep thinking these distressing ideas and images.	*Just like Michaela said, I worry about things I haven't done or won't do. Psychopaths don't worry about many of the things they've done.*
I could physically stab her.	*I don't want to because I know I'm a good person who doesn't act out bad thoughts.*

Experience #9:
What about caregivers?

Example
From Michaela's point of view

Being a caregiver of someone with OCD isn't an easy task and certainly isn't for the faint of heart. It has taken many years of patience and understanding to live with OCD being so prevalent in our married life. For many years, I felt like a small boat being tossed in the middle of the sea during a hurricane, waiting to see if the next wave would be the one to come crashing down on everything, ending our relationship.

The truth is, you aren't alone. It can be freeing to find someone who understands what you're going through or a support group whose members can put themselves in your shoes. A few years back, I was introduced to a spouse whose partner suffered from the same obsessions as David. Talking to another person who understood took a burden off of me and allowed me to realize there were other caregivers out there carrying similar burdens.

Being in a relationship with someone who has OCD is about always being prepared for anything. It's about padding in extra time for compulsions while balancing them with the reality that we live on a time schedule. Ultimately, I have learned to anticipate what may come up on any given day and try to counterbalance it with something that will not act as a trigger or stimuli for David. I have also learned to resist the temptation to facilitate the obsessions and compulsions that are OCD. As we have continued our relationship, I feel more confident that I can confront the OCD head-on while working together with David as a united front, so the obsessive-compulsive cycles aren't so prevalent.

What the Research Says

OCD occupies time, energy, and trust in any relationship—particularly marriage. Scholarly research indicates the result of responding to obsessive-compulsive cycles can be a significant degree of disruption of daily life:

> [A survey]...of family members of adults with OCD...reported that 75% experienced disruption in their lives because of the OCD, including loss of personal relationships, loss of leisure time, and financial problems...approximately 75% of OCD relatives participated at least minimally in rituals or avoidance or modified their behavior to accommodate patients' symptoms. (Steketee & Van Noppen, 2004, p. 59)

In other words, caregivers experience tremendous challenges that are shared with their partners. They are never alone.

Didonna identifies OCD as a trust disorder in that people who suffer from OCD cannot trust what they do, what their senses tell them, or what they remember. Following a triggering moment, people with OCD shift into "automatic pilot" and react by performing rituals to reduce the anxiety they feel. Didonna continues to explain that people who have OCD ask those around them for reassurance. Ironically, this reassurance that is received by others feeds and strengthens the obsessive problems and increases the person's insecurity and distrust of themselves. As tough as it can be for a partner to ignore, reassurance offers temporary relief that continues to feed the obsession.

Tips for Healing

OCD is the third person in our marriage. I recognize that by marrying David, I married his OCD as well. When I compare the two "parts" of David, I realize that his OCD inserts itself in our marriage like a major storm that comes out of nowhere during a midwestern summer. Strong marriages take constant work, and marriages with the addition of OCD make the work even more challenging and critical.

We have a name for David's OCD that has become a part of our vocabulary—Herb. We chose this name to lessen the emotional effects of OCD on our marriage by using humor. We mean no offense to anyone who has that name; it's just the name we chose. By personifying OCD, we can agree through our implicit trust for each other that Herb is not David. Herb is a part of David, and we have both agreed that Herb is not welcome in our relationship. A result of this agreement is a mutual goal to prevent Herb from taking over our marriage.

When it comes to surviving a serious disorder such as OCD, we use a lot of humor in our relationship to keep the disorder in perspective. This is not to mean that we solely use humor. Humor is just one tool in our kit that helps us to lessen the effects of OCD in our marriage. Using humor helps us to keep in mind that the OCD will not have power over us. David's OCD is separate from him and is not who he is. Naming the OCD assists me in telling David that Herb is "doing it." I have found by addressing the cycles this way, I am not attacking my partner as a person as much as I am reminding him that Herb has taken control at that moment. When traveling, we joke about leaving Herb back at home since he tends to be a bit of a killjoy. This way, when David starts "doing it" (obsessions or compulsions), I can gently remind him that we left Herb at home.

As difficult as it may be, it has been helpful in our marriage to confront the obsessions and compulsions directly. It may seem simple to give in to the obsessions and compulsions, but everyone loses when accommodating cycles. I have worked with David to be more sympathetic by learning about the different therapies and supporting him as he deals with the daily challenges of OCD. Educating ourselves about OCD has been a key part in combating the disorder.

We Felt Alone but We Weren't

Having OCD as a married couple can feel like living on an island—until you realize you aren't alone. In this first part of this book, we have shared our story, established a baseline definition of the disorder, discussed levels of awareness, and illustrated some hot topics we have experienced. This comprehensive review of our experience shows how you can, as a loving couple, commit to own your OCD and live life more fully. Telling your story can be a bold first step in this direction. In the next section, we will break down this healing process into bite-sized pathways.

Six Ways to
REBUILD
Your Marriage

Key Objectives

This section intends to help you:

- understand the six pathways of the model

- consider how you can apply the model to improve your marriage

- evaluate the action plans you implement

- build further confidence to seek help and continuously maintain your relationship

- review interactive exercises to reflect how you can apply these concepts in your relationship

Chapter 8
Pathway One
Cultivate Empathy for Your Spouse

I FLED Him, down the nights and down the days;
I fled Him, down the arches of the years;
I fled Him, down the labyrinthine ways
Of my own mind; and in the mist of tears
I hid from Him, and under running laughter.

— Francis Thompson, *Hound of Heaven*

Coping with OCD in a marriage can seem like being chased by a predator trapped in one's mind. Thompson's (1917) description aptly portrays this initial struggle of acute stress response, between flying from our true identity and guiding spirit to actively fighting the shadows of our personalities. Having a conceptual model with which to combat this threat can be useful and can support healing a relationship over long periods of time. As mentioned at the beginning of this book, we chose to use Melissa Orlov's (2010) 6-Step Model for healing relationships because we saw it was helpful for couples who are dealing with ADHD. Since this book is based on our experiences with OCD, we modified her ADHD model to a non-sequential pathway construct that can be entered anywhere along the path.[32]

---

32. You can read more about ADHD and relationships in *The ADHD Effect on Marriage* (2010), or visit Orlov's website at adhdmarriage.com.

The 6-Pathway Model in Figure 8.1 is user friendly because a person can enter the process at any place in the figure to begin to improve the relationship. The end result is empathetic communication. We can build strong relationships that result in enhanced trust. By actively listening and talking to each other, we can better respond to each other's needs, and be more empathetic. As we travel through life, there is no certain path that leads us on our journey. There are no arrows in the figure because each path informs each other in any direction. Anyone, at any time, can choose or not choose a particular path—or even 'merge' more than one simultaneously. No one has to take any particular path in any sequence. In this section, we will describe the general characteristics of each path, consider applications of their principles from our perspective as a married couple living with obsessive-compulsive disorder (OCD), and present some strategies with which married couples can confront the inherent challenges.

Table 8.1

Orlov's 6-Pathway Model

Path 1: Cultivate Empathy for Spouse

Path 6: Rebalance & Reignite Romance

Path 2: Address Emotions

EVALUATE

Path 5: Find Your Voices

Path 3: Improve Communication

Path 4: Get Treatment for Both

Countering the effect of OCD on marriage.
Like other models that address anxiety disorders (e.g., Orlov's (2010) six steps for ADHD), this model lays out a discrete way to cope with OCD in any marriage. Unlike other models, it provides iterative, linked pathways (i.e., one can voluntarily start at any point and move around as one wishes) and is not exclusively sequential (i.e., can go in any direction), emphasizes empathy and communication in relationships, describes self-evaluation as a continuous and reflective process, and inserts the concept of regaining life balance. For sequential learners, following the numbered paths can offer a logical start point for the healing process.

Trust in marriage is grounded in empathy for one another. Trust is confidence in another person, that the person will be there for the partner and the relationship no matter what. Empathy is more than putting oneself in another's place; it is the building block for a foundation of love and can be the difference between harmful and constructive behavior in a family.[33]

An example from our own experiences illustrates the value of empathy within the context of trust. As a person with primarily obsessive thoughts that emphasize sexual-violent taboos, I have regularly cycled about stabbing Michaela and/or pushing her downstairs. The thoughts can be vivid. The blood seems real. Even more intense and present is the fear that I might just do these things. Yet, in over twenty-five years of marriage, I've done none of these things. By understanding that these thoughts are symptoms of a disorder rather than valid manifestations of my personality, Michaela has learned to push back without accepting the obsessions—often with sarcasm. The dialogue below mimics conversations we have had countless times. Notes in brackets indicate key insights we have gained pertaining to my pervasive cycles of obsessive thoughts feeding compulsions to confess to Michaela. While it may seem abnormal, the pain and fear behind the words were very real for the first 10-15 years of our marriage. Through time, we have both learned to lean on our humor, communication, and—most of all—trust to cope with less frequent compulsive interactions.

> **DAVID:** *I have a knife in my hand and just imagined that I stabbed you in the back of the neck* [typical cycle of an uncommanded, obsessive thought leading to a compulsive confession].
>
> **MICHAELA:** *Well, you're not. I would stab you first* [programmed sarcastic response that jabs back and relies on humor—instead of physical retribution—that aligns with the couple's personality].

---

33. For more details on trust, see Covey, 2006 and May, 2004. For more information on empathy and relationships, see Paradiso-Michau, 2018 and Brown, 2001.

DAVID: *But… aren't I terrible? Doesn't that mean I don't really love you, that we're incompatible? …. Maybe we should get divorced* [while less frequent now, I sometimes fall back on this defensive illogic of snowballing when I'm really tired or sick].

MICHAELA: *You're doing it* [her way of saying I'm cycling, an agreed-upon term we use to communicate in the midst of an otherwise irrational act]! Stop!

DAVID: OK…. *Hmmmmpf* […not liking it because it takes energy to snap out of the cycle. But we have built trust in empathy over time, so I know Michaela has my best interests at heart when she commands that I break the cycle. Yes, it gets easier to do over time].

✷An action plan for this pathway might include activities that build up empathetic trust:

- **Develop a nonverbal communication method.** For example, we often squeeze our hands three times to mean "I-love-you"— anytime, anywhere.

- **Pray and/or meditate together to facilitate a sense of common experiences.** We just started doing this by listening to a daily meditation podcast. It has taken Michaela twenty years to get to this point of trust because of my spontaneous hand-laying prayer cycles in public when we were first married.

- **Conduct regular activities of communication.** With teleworking during the COVID 19 pandemic of 2020, we walked every day and had the most natural, free-flowing conversations about both mundane and significant topics. Perhaps more importantly, I wasn't compulsively briefing Michaela from a meticulously detailed list which I have done daily for much of the quarter-century. What better way is there to be present for each other?

Chapter 9
Pathway Two
Address Emotions
in the Relationship

Emotions play an important role in any relationship, particularly a marriage with OCD. Emotions are not only feelings; they weigh down specific thoughts (obsessions) that result in behaviors (compulsions) that provide a sense of short-term relief…until the next cycle begins. Pathway Two logically links the need for empathy (Pathway One) and communication (Pathway Three), foundations for building lifelong trust. Quite often, married couples must shift their paradigms from old individual habits of thought to new patterns of constructing meaning together.[34] Changing paradigms will result in an openness to being heart-centered and a willingness to address key emotions. Two major elements of OCD in our marriage have been

---

34. Orlov (2010) discusses how acknowledging and addressing emotions can strengthen relationships.

frustration from a lack of awareness and fear of intrusive thoughts that make us question our identity as a couple.

Mindfulness, an awareness of self and the couple's relationship, has enabled us to accept our shortcomings as individuals and as a couple. We have incorporated mindfulness primarily by practicing empathy and meditation. Just being present to one another can generate empathy. Observing others' emotions may trigger similar neurobiological responses in the observers, particularly in the anterior cortex and pulse (Hofmann, Grossman, & Hinton, 2011). The biophysical response to empathic behavior has enabled us to open to each other, especially when we have a hard time understanding the other's perspective. Meditative practice can also enable us to be more accepting of ourselves. Meditation can complement cognitive-behavioral treatment (CBT) and enhance psychological and neuroendocrine benefits by enabling patients to mindfully experience the present (Hofmann et al., 2011). Emerging evidence suggests that meditative practices can enhance attentiveness, positivity, and empathy while reducing negative emotions (Hofmann et al., 2011). While more research is needed to address the benefits of meditation, we have found that attending contemplative retreats and listening to contemplative podcasts at night can help us wind down together after hectic days/weeks. Finding a meditative practice we feel comfortable doing together has been a twenty-five-year journey.

Obsessive thoughts in our marriage have emotional tags. For me as a virtual "Pure-O," obsessions are vibrant and colorful—the more taboo and destructive, the more vibrant and colorful. Baer (2002) defines bad thoughts as "thinking the most inappropriate things at the most inappropriate times" (p. xiv). Put another way, obsessions often arise at the worst times, further highlighting the emotional insecurity. This intensity of obsessions has led me to wonder if they are legitimate and to question my own identity and goodness as a human being for decades—regardless of my impeccable behavior. Additionally, a need for symmetry, a seemingly comfortable balance between good and bad, has occasionally led me to respond to perceived insults with righteous indignation. Baer (2002) explains how insidious and pervasive OCD can be because it latches on to any taboos we perceive. These bad thoughts can convince us that we are bad people who will carry out these bad behaviors.

Clinicians have long realized that thoughts do not control our behavior.

But the very facts that she [an OCD sufferer] feels guilty and worries about having such awful thoughts, and that she has never physically harmed anyone before, are all the clues I [a clinician] need to be able to reassure her that she is not a murderess, but rather one of millions of people who suffer in silence from bad thoughts. (Baer, 2002, p. xiv)

> **Clinicians have long realized that thoughts do not control our behavior.**

In fact, it's normal to have abnormal thoughts. "You are not as abnormal as you think. Every human being is visited from time to time by the … most inappropriate thoughts at the most inappropriate times" (Baer, 2002, p. 6). Put another way, people who are bothered by disturbing thoughts are often convinced they may possibly act them out (Baer, 2002). But, as Michaela reminded me many years ago, the fact that I worry about those thoughts I have never acted upon means I'm normal. I'd be in trouble if I committed the behaviors and didn't worry about that. Finally, Baer (2002) observes that past behavior, not thoughts, predicts future behavior:

…the very fact that they have never acted on their thoughts and urges up until now is an excellent predictor that they will never act

on them. A rock-solid axiom of both psychology and criminology is that the best predictor of future behavior is past behavior. (p. 37, italics in original)

Emotions play a role in marriages that have an OCD component, but being mindful of the insidious nature of obsessive thoughts coupled with a keen need for symmetry can help open minds and console uncertain sufferers that they are, in fact, good people. As a happy result, thoughts do not necessarily predict behavior.

✴An action plan for this pathway might include activities that build up mindfulness and counter obsessive thoughts:

- **Establish a habit of meditative practice that enables you, individually at first and then as a couple if possible, to become more self-aware.** My awareness that I was driven by anger became clear to me through Tai Chi and Centering Prayer. It was only after I became aware of that part of me that I deliberately set out to replace that anger with love. As a result, I have learned how to better let go of past anxieties with false identities and to embrace the present.[35] I can now open my mind to the possibility that perceived injustices may just be miscommunications that don't require righteous responses. That has made all the difference in me and my approach to our married life.

- **Employ validated practices to break the cycle of obsessive thinking.** Your partner can alert you to your cycling, but you have to resolve to take the first step. I have found the 4-step method[36] very

---

35. Culkin, 2016, 2019; Tolle, 1999/2010.
36. Schwartz & Beyette, 1996/2016, describe the 4-step model to help reclaim one's life and thinking patterns from OCD.

effective in especially relabeling and reattributing obsessive thoughts as what they are: attributes of a neuropsychiatric disorder that I can control. See the full discussion of this method in the next pathway.

- **Write in a personal journal in any medium to capture your responses to and reflections of obsessions.** While this practice can make you feel vulnerable, it can also strengthen your resolve, clarify the difference between rational and irrational experiences, and help you envision a way forward.[37] There is so much *gray* to experience as opposed to the black-white symmetric world that many with OCD inhabit.

> **Now that we have explored how empathy and emotional mindfulness can lead to openness, we are ready to examine communication in the next pathway.**

---

37. To see an example of how writing about your lived experiences with OCD can help you heal, review my dissertation and its synopsis (Culkin, 2016, 2019).

Chapter 10
Pathway Three
Improve
Communication

Communication in a marriage occurs at many levels. As our marriage has matured, we have developed multiple layers of communication channels to convey what's in our hearts and our minds—much of which we choose to never convey to anyone else. For us, communication is the lifeline of our relationship. When I have compulsively assaulted that lifeline—through daily briefing sessions, failing to actively listen to Michaela, and talking over her—it has damaged the communication in our marriage. In this sense, quality communication stems from the previous two pathways (regarding empathy and emotions) and is necessary for behavior to improve in other pathways (seeking help, finding a voice, rebalancing, etc.). The short story that follows illustrates the complexity of communication in our marriage, and a subsequent action plan suggests some helpful techniques to improve communication.

We enjoy traveling with one another to experience and explore new places. Traveling over the years has forced us to realize that my tolerance for change and security requirements is limited. (For example, I was told on a recent overseas business trip to be flexible because the itinerary would likely change hour-to-hour—this scenario is *just not* in the OCD playbook.) By day seven of a more recent trip we took together, my patience was worn thin. I was not in my usual place (home) with my usual routine. I was happy to stay in a new "vacation routine" that was working for me, and I wasn't feeling flexible. Michaela and I had chosen to walk along the downtown strip during the hustle of the evening rush on stores for food and trinkets. Of course, instead of enjoying the present moment with Michaela, I was stuck on feeling sorry for myself for doing what she wanted (although I had agreed to join her for dessert) and not having completed my own personal agenda of somewhat compulsive activities for that day. I was projecting the inflated importance of my preferences upon my closest loved one, my wife and caregiver, without regard for her needs. My obsessive thinking followed my typical illogic that I must tell her all my troublesome thoughts to ensure we communicate about everything (the 'same' as quality communication in my warped universe) so that our trust and therefore our relationship did not collapse. In other words, I convinced myself at these times that not telling Michaela what's on my mind would inevitably lead to divorce. Of course, being the strong-willed-I-won't-put-up-with-Herb character that she is (one of many things I love about her), she walked off without warning to buy me the food I had told her I wanted. I was determined to get what I wanted, in spite of our location in a beautiful part of the world. I wound up waiting where she left me for over an hour before going back to the hotel room. Luckily, she was there safe. I, however, paid lip service to her safety and selfishly unleashed my anger about the lack of communication, that I would never hear the end of it from family and friends if something had happened to her, and that I wouldn't have waited for her on the street if I hadn't cared. I, I, I. Me. Me. Me. She let me unload, and then we went to sleep in the separate beds in the hotel room. The next morning, I saw the following text (Figure 10.1).

Figure 10.1
Michaela's text to me after an OCD cycle

Dave,

I can tell how angry you are right now and honestly, I understand. I think your feelings are pretty much akin to how I felt when I came back to the room and you weren't there. I, myself, even walked around the hotel a few times to look for you, and I even decided to ask the police for help if you weren't back by a certain time. Honestly, it made me feel sad to think I had left my battle buddy, and a little mad at myself that I had left you on your own in the big city. This isn't about anyone else…it's about us. It's about us being too old to play games…and, if were are honest with one another, we were playing a stupid game tonight…not just me, but both of us.

Honestly, my feelings were bruised that you knew what you were getting into tonight, yet you played your own game of complaining when I asked you to go get dessert with me. My feelings were hurt when you said your day wasn't your own and was dictated for you.

So here we are at a standoff - you're mad and I'm by myself…something I often feel…that I'm by myself. It's not about who is right and wrong. It's about being battle buddies and supporting one another.

…so go to bed…sweet dreams…I won't have you in another situation where you have to worry about me.

Texting your true self is communicating.

In one text, Michaela taught me a lot about communication. Rather than assigning blame, she focuses on our shared responsibility to make this relationship work. Without being mocking or cynical, she explains that she cares while refusing to be rolled over by the irrational bull of my OCD. And notice how her civil, rational tone effectively conveys her message without kowtowing to my passionate indignation of the moment. As a result, I calmed down and we had an intense, yet productive, discussion that morning. In calm language, each of us listened to the other and pointed out what we were/not thinking at various points during the previous night. After an hour, we both felt somewhat relieved by the cathartic talk, more confident that we had confronted the demon that Herb can manifest himself to be. We could look forward to enjoying the present moment together on our vacation once again. We could move forward as a stronger couple.

Going through this deliberate, rational process of honest communication has helped us counter many of the effects of the irrational cycles of OCD. The process centers on our true identities as husband and wife, rather than two egos trapped in an endless cycle in a specific time and place. We could have had this fierce conversation anywhere and any day. What matters is that we both continue to choose to work things out. We do that by communicating and reminding ourselves that we love each other.

✶An action plan for this pathway might include activities that improve communication skills while building upon other skill sets such as empathy and emotional intelligence:

- As educators, we have found certain assessment tools to be effective in improving personal communication skills. Genetics and neurobiology, rather than family upbringing, cause OCD; as a result, non-judgmental communication is critical to healing inter- and intra-personal relationships (Hyman & Pedrick, 1999). Learning audits, for example, are simple questions we can ask ourselves and each other to discern our blind spots. What did I learn from today that I didn't know before? How can it help improve my marriage? Why was my partner angry at me—from his/her perspective? How can I empathize with that view and reconcile it with my own?

- Use a behavioral tracker to help you become more aware of triggers and compulsive behaviors. After all, looking at concrete data can help a person discover different triggers over a period of time. Using the matrix in Figure 10.2 helped me become more aware of the frequency and intensity of anger in our marriage, once we were diagnosed. Indeed, diagnosis opened a new world of tools we could use to fight OCD.[38]

Figure 10.2
David's behavioral tracker of angry responses

DATE	LISTEN TO KAY	HURTFUL COMMENTS	DESTRUCTIVE ANGER	REMARKS
31 May		1 – faithfulness		breaths CHILL OUT!
1 June			1 – laptop	breaths
2 June			1x threw keys	breaths
3 June	30 min			
4		1		
5		1		acted grave and determined to change
9	20 min	1		chill out; frustrated at kids
12	20 min	1		talked about gym
13			1	combined calendars
14	10 min			forest; tired
15	10			impatient, breaths

- Be satisfied you've done your best in the given circumstances.
- Take time outs.
- Look beyond emotion to seek the message.
- Chill out! Relax—mentally & physically.
- Have confidence that you're a good person.
- Don't scope out other women and focus on Kaela.
- Cut down on hurtful comments—show HONOR.
- Be your own best friend.
- Continue to take TIME OUTS—from worries and MADE UP problems.

38. See Hyman & Pedrick, 1999 and Schwartz & Beyette, 1996/2016.

- Write in a personal journal in any medium to capture your responses to and reflections of obsessions. Writing is an effective means for self-talk and counterpunching obsessive thoughts. For instance, I could write down an obsessive thought about an attractive actress I have seen in a movie. The obsession would possibly involve a snowball of illogically connected images: stalking her, running away with her, divorcing Michaela, etc. The counterpunch would involve reality if I acted on the obsession: get a restraining order for stalking, her not paying me the time of day, Michaela's heart being broken, etc. Writing down the counterpunches helped me to see just how irrational I was being.

- Re-write your wedding vows, here and now. This can be a powerful exercise to remind each other how grateful you are for your partner and not to take each other for granted. Writing forces you to logically think through an important commitment—rather than impulsively surmise illogical assumptions with little basis in reality. We did this in the eighth year of our marriage as illustrated in Figure 10.3. What a good way to celebrate Valentine's Day!

Figure 10.3
An example of David's re-written marriage vows

Renewed Marriage Vows

1. I will love and honor you forever. Respect will flow between us and out to others.

2. I will not hang on to guilt, but I will remember the scars of previous wounds to change my behavior constructively and thereby take responsibility for my current actions.

3. I will serve others together with you, my family.

4. I will put your needs above mine.

5. I will smile more and open my heart in the spirit of sharing, faith, trust, and hope. I will share/pursue my dreams with you and yours.

6. I will listen to you and tell you how I feel - be honest with you and myself.

7. I will refrain from unjust judgment and impatience.

Chapter 11

Pathway Four
Get Treatment
for Both of You

For many couples, deciding to get treatment is terrifying; yet, it can mean the difference between divorce or remaining married. For us, OCD is an existential threat to our marriage. In this pathway, the foundation of trust built through empathy (Pathway One), emotional awareness (Pathway Two), and improved communications (Pathway Three) is paramount. When partners trust each other implicitly with their lives, they are ready to make such an impactful choice. We will describe how we experienced the nature and treatment of OCD in our married life so that it may resonate with your own.

When our therapist diagnosed me with OCD, it was a relief. We had known for some time there was something wrong. That we couldn't name it made me question if I was a bad person by nature. The diagnosis changed all that. We both could now put a name to the disorder and learn about it so we could cope with it. We could now know our opponent. Initially, we had the same social preconceptions about OCD that others perceive – stereotypes like being neurotic, a neat freak, germaphobic, and perfectionistic. This misperception meant that my particular symptoms—the constant checking, uncommanded thoughts on sexual—violent taboos that wouldn't stop, extreme self-doubt, incapacity to deal with external stimuli (yes, I yelled at a blue jay once for interrupting my homework solitude), religious scrupulosity, and the need to brief meticulous lists to my wife—now had a root cause. I hadn't realized how much OCD had pervaded our life together. I was no longer a bad person. This relief we felt from receiving a diagnosis preceded decades of very hard work, without which—we are convinced—we would not still be married.

The treatment of OCD has been established for some time, but the nature of the disorder often remains misunderstood. Koen and Stein (2015) describe the basic characteristics and treatments of OCD. "OCD is widely conceptualized as a neuropsychiatric disorder, in which dysfunctional neural circuitry and neurochemical changes culminate in characteristic symptomatology" (Koen & Stein, 2015, p. 622). As a result, clinicians often use cognitive-behavioral therapy (CBT), sometimes coupled with medications such as serotonin-specific reuptake inhibitors (SSRI), to treat the neuro-biological elements. Other treatment techniques can include reflection, narrative review, and journaling to augment existing plans to foster self-confidence when patients can feel very vulnerable.[39] Of course, improving lifestyle in terms of diet, exercise, and hygienic sleep can also foster an individual's and a couples' resilience in concert with more traditional treatment options.[40] We had determined from the beginning that we would seek treatment together because it was our disorder to confront.

The form of CBT most effective for us was exposure and response prevention (ERP). The premise is that one calls to mind a trigger for an obsession and then gradually builds up a tolerance to responding

39. Kunz, 2007; Weg, 2011.
40. Orlov, 2010.

to it with a corresponding compulsion—thereby breaking the cycle. For example, I would record all of my most horrifying obsessions and their implications on a tape recorder. I would then listen to them over and over again. (It is important to mention that Michaela and I agreed that she would never listen to what I was recording. These recordings were just for me to listen to as part of my ERP.) For me, running someone over, hurting a person, or stabbing Michaela were top contenders. Listening to these in one 10–minute session was, at first, extremely difficult. At first, I couldn't make it. I sweated profusely and actually shook to my core out of well-habituated fear and doubt. Then, after doing this for several days, I realized I could get through the script. Soon after, I realized I wasn't doing my compulsions to prevent these obsessions from coming to fruition: checking under the car, briefing Michaela, confessing my obsessions to a priest, saying certain prayers a certain number of times to 'repent.' It was while going through this exhausting process that I could convince myself that maybe I did not have to do my compulsions and that the obsessions did not mean I would take any of the actions I most feared.

✳An action plan for this pathway might include activities that build up confidence to seek help together:

- Use available resources to learn about mental health providers in the local area who are experienced in OCD diagnosis and treatment. Not all providers are. The International Obsessive-Compulsive Disorder Foundation (IOCDF, 2020) has a wide spectrum of resources available in one place at http://www.iocdf.org.[41]

- Read about ERP and other treatment options to learn how you may apply them in your marriage. It is a preferred treatment for many with OCD and has even demonstrated positive results in internet and app-based modes. I read about ERP and developed a quick reference (see Figure 11.1) that I carried in my wallet for years. In the heat of an obsessive thought, I could remind myself that my

---

41. You can read more about therapies and medications later in this book (Chapter 17).

obsessions (Relabel) were grounded in a neurochemical disorder (Reattribute) and that I could choose positive behaviors (Refocus) to detract from the emotional tag of the obsessive thoughts (Revalue). This took some time, but it was worth it.[42]

• Continue to write in a personal journal in any medium to capture your responses to and reflections of obsessions. Journaling helped mitigate my symptoms. Writing your story can make you feel vulnerable, but it can also strengthen your resolve, heighten your commitment to make sense of your fragmented identity, clarify the difference between rational and irrational experiences, and help you envision a way forward through therapy.[43] Put another way, journaling has helped me become more mindful of my symptoms, relive triggers in a safe and controlled way, and gain some cognitive-emotional control by reframing my role in our relationship story.

Figure 11.1

I share this as part of what I did to help me with the different steps of ERP. This example is meant to illustrate something you can do to combat your own OCD by filling in your own content.

Some OCD Observations
(Reference: Brain Lock by Schwartz, 1996)

1. **My responsibilities in our family relationship:** use tapes for my ERP, read love letter from Michaela for reassurance, circle most important comments to cut down on brief list, take my medications, and trust Michaela's feedback about cycling.

2. **4-Step Method for ERP:** Break the cycle and recognize the thoughts/obsessions that are due to OCD (biochemical), and then perform a constructive activity that I enjoy for at least 15 minutes in lieu of performing a compulsion. Realize that it is OCD that I have.

---

42. See Patel et al., 2018 and Roncero et al., 2018 for more details about ERP treatment options for OCD. For my wallet card, I used the model from Schwartz & Beyette, 1996/2016. Yes, it was in a very small font size!

43. For more information on how I used my personal story to make sense of our experience of living and surviving with OCD, check out my dissertation and its synopsis article (Culkin, 2016, 2019).

It's not me or a character flaw. In Relabeling and Reattributing, I'm asking, "Why am I doing this?" Be mindfully aware of what I'm thinking and doing in response. Daily meditation can help in this and help ground me physically mentally, and spiritually. Write down significant changes and observations in trends. Realize I am NOT the center of everything; not everyone or everything is against me. Schwartz & Beyette (1996) note that...no one ever does anything morally objectionable because of OCD. I am not going to act out my obsession. I won't lose control although I may fear losing control. "It doesn't take over your will." Past performance is the best measure of the future....

a. **RELABEL immediately as:**

　i. *OBSESSION:* intrusive thought, idea, rumination, phrase, word, image

　　　1. Types: violent, avoid good-looking women, hurting loved one, hurt self, scrupulosity, blaming self, paranoia, reassurance questions, inappropriate reception of constructive criticism

　　　2. Excuses: false wish, empty apology, anger, introversion

　ii. *ANXIETY:* Temporary; characterized by guilt and sadness. Doubt; worry about worries

　iii. *COMPULSION:* May be *mental* (righteous feeling, perceived need, rumination, counting, rearranging, briefing/writing list, reassurance questions). Can also be *visible* (brief list, circle comments, wince, checking). Overdoing (documentation, "virtuous acts," prayer)

b. **REATTRIBUTE.** Realize this may be a medical condition due to a biochemical imbalance in my brain which results in receiving false, garbage messages. It's not me; it's OCD. Blame it on the brain. I can't be responsible for the thoughts that enter my brain, but I am responsible for what I do in response and for getting treatment.

   i. ANTICIPATE: Prepare for obsessions and situations that produce them. Be ready to blame the brain and not follow the obsession.

   ii. ACCEPT: Say the Serenity Prayer. Retain my poise and stature and self-esteem. It's not *because* of me but *despite* me that this occurs.

c. REFOCUS. Turn the other cheek, and do another, pleasurable, wholesome behavior—for example, a hobby—for at least 15 minutes (waiting at least 15 minutes and then perhaps, if able, attempting to delay for another period—*15-minute rule*). Delay or ignore compulsions: draw in pencil, work out, take a walk with family, hike, pastels, write poems, read. Remember, these are truly false messages. It's not how I feel in response to the obsessions; it's what I do in response that counts. The more I change my behavior utilizing my WILL, the more my thoughts (brain chemistry) may change.

d. REVALUE. Devalue the false messages. Who cares if they don't go away? They're not real anyway. Use humor. Reality doesn't mimic OCD feelings; the degree to which I accept what/who I am measures my success as a person. **IF IT FEELS LIKE IT MIGHT BE OCD, IT IS OCD.** The more clearly I see what OCD symptoms are, the more rapidly I can dismiss them as worthless garbage and not pay attention to them.

After you seek professional help and begin treatment, the next task involves finding a voice—both as individuals and as a couple.

Chapter 12
Pathway Five
Find Your Voice(s)

This pathway involves finding a voice as both an individual and as a married couple coping with OCD. 'Finding a voice' essentially means discerning one's true identity as a husband, a wife, a lover, a friend, a caregiver, and/or a patient. To illustrate this process, I will describe my dissertation journey and suggest some specific activities for an action plan.

I chose to write an autoethnographic dissertation because I had to heal. Autoethnography involves writing rich and compelling narratives about one's own lived experiences within a specific culture in order to give voice to an individual who would otherwise not be heard.[44] Living with OCD for over 30 years and having it almost destroy my marriage convinced me that I had to do something. When

44. Culkin, 2016, 2019; Schwandt, 2015. A dissertation is a capstone written research report to complete the requirements of a doctorate or terminal professional degree.

I took my first qualitative research methodology course in the fall of 2013, I knew I had found the tools whereby I could begin to pick up the puzzle pieces of my identity. OCD's pervasive obsessions had patiently picked at my egotistical identity over the years without realizing it. In this sense, OCD had unknowingly become a third person in our marriage: an enemy within whom we called 'Herb.' I reviewed over 2,000 pages of raw data from my journals, grandfather's autobiography, and personal correspondence to identify certain life events that triggered my response. These life events consisted of significant emotional moments such as the deaths of my parents within six months of one another, being diagnosed with OCD, and finding a peaceful way to practice my faith while avoiding scrupulosity. From a broader perspective, I analyzed the stories of these life events at the intersection of three primary themes: coping with death, healing from mental illness, and seeking spiritual development. As a result, I could pick up the puzzle pieces of my identity over time and refashion them into an integrated narrative representing the identity I have constructed. When I defended the dissertation, it was the most vulnerable I had ever felt because I was announcing my OCD to a world that held the disorder in a prejudged mold. Please see the next figure that depicts the spiral model of autoethnography I used to help express this journey. That said, it was a wonderfully empowering experience for the same reason.

✳An action plan for this pathway might include activities that create spaces in which you can reflect on identity and the expression of that identity:

- Write your own story as a married couple living with OCD. How did you find out you had it? Why did you decide to seek help? What obstacles did you overcome during therapy? What obstacles have you yet to overcome? Answering these and related questions not only records a version of your life narrative but also allows you to show yourselves how much you have developed as individuals and as a couple over the course of your marriage. Narrative is a powerful means to look under the multiple layers of ego we all accumulate over our lifetimes in order to find our true identities.[45]

- Mindfulness and meditative practices previously discussed can amplify self-awareness. This experience can facilitate the identification of one's strengths and weaknesses during therapy and personal conversations. During therapy, we found it helpful when I could describe what was 'going on in my head' during specific obsessive-compulsive cycles. This allowed the therapist to suggest particularly helpful homework and enabled Michaela to better understand my state of mind in the throes of irrational cycling.

- Seek out arts-based modes of expression. Local poetry, crafts, and writing workshops afford opportunities to develop personal skills that can harness our creative energies. What is more, such collaborative ventures can open you and your partner to other ways people live through similar experiences. Figure 12.1 on next page illustrates how I used a spiral model to express my OCD journey for my dissertation process.

> **Having holistically addressed the marriage relationship from several angles in Pathways One–Five, the culmination of the model involves strengthening the marriage bond itself.**

45. In my dissertation, I examine how narratives have helped me heal over time at the intersection of coping with death, struggling to develop spiritually, and living with a mental disorder (Culkin, 2016, 2019). Weg (2011) specifically investigates how narratives can facilitate living with OCD.

Figure 12.1
Spiral concept

Illustration concept by D. Culkin.

Chapter 13
Pathway Six
Rebalance and Reignite Romance

"Herb," our moniker for the despised OCD ego in our marriage, forces us to have better communication. I'll admit it. Michaela and I have learned to channel the passion Herb has for taboos and bugging the heck out of both of us. Herb tries to reprioritize our perspectives of what's important. He transforms my fear of uncertainty into a concrete doubt as to whether or not I'm satisfying her. An openness to balance and romance has come largely through awareness, empathetic communication, and hard work in therapy—the ultimate integration of the other five pathways of the model.

Awareness has become a key component of rebalancing and reprioritizing our lives as a married couple. Before we were diagnosed, we knew something was wrong. We couldn't name it or address it. With diagnosis came professional treatment. We shifted from unwilling ignorance to willful learning—anything we could—about OCD. As we learned more about the disorder, we realized that we were not alone. Other people shared very similar experiences online, in self-help sessions, and in workbooks. This search for knowledge became a need to heal, the title of my dissertation.[46] These experiences have led us on a path not only of self-discovery but also one to help others. When we presented our OCD journey at a local church, it was a watershed moment. We realized how cathartic it was to share our story and, by so doing, heal ourselves and help others. In this sense, OCD awareness has marked our transformation from a struggling married couple to one that actively reaches out to other sufferers.

This awareness has promoted empathy in developing the communication in our relationship. As discussed in Pathways One and Two, selfless concern and care for each other (empathy) drive trust in a marriage. Obsession-compulsion cycles can isolate a sufferer, placing him in a cocoon of obsession that is immune to most attempts at communication by the partner. As a result of this self-imposed oppression, the couple must leave the door open a crack to the possibility of normalcy. In this context, awareness that cycling is wrong and excessive is the first step toward admitting there is a problem in the marriage that requires tending. We recognize that it is a difficult, but necessary, step to seek help.

Our therapy has included ERP, medication, and trust and has facilitated the holistic application of the other pathways. In two words, the journey has been *very difficult*. That said, I would not change anything for the world because the journey has also empowered us to never take each other for granted. One day during the early therapy sessions, our therapist asked me a simple but daunting question: What would you do if Michaela left you because of OCD? I hadn't thought of that possibility before. The question felt

---

46. See Culkin, 2016. As I am nervous of self-plagiarizing, I have erred on the side of caution by, perhaps compulsively, over-footnoting.

like an invading army surrounding the moat of a castle that protects my secrets and most precious feelings: my ego. How could my wife think of leaving me when I was the one who was "broken?"[47] My selfish cocoon had made it difficult for me to see our marital challenges from her perspective. Fortunately, this experience triggered my awareness and a need to trust in Michaela's feedback. While we still struggle occasionally—because the OCD has never completely receded—the frequency and intensity has lessened over time with a lot of patience and practice.

✳An action plan for this pathway might include activities that create spaces in which you can reflect on your family priorities, romance, and creativity:

- Write your own love story. Establish yourselves as the main characters. What chain of events leads to your meeting? To falling in love? How do you overcome challenges to that love? Be funny and have fun with writing a story that you can make as real or made up as you both like.

- Meditation can calm the senses and amplify sensitivity to mindfulness. Becoming aware of your current state can enable you to realize what is really important and reprioritize accordingly. How will your love life improve when you place your partner in the center?

- Seek out arts-based modes of expression to enhance the senses. Local poetry, crafts, and writing workshops afford opportunities to develop personal skills that can harness your creative energies. What is more, such collaborative ventures can open you and your partner to other ways people live through similar experiences. By enhancing your sensual experiences together, you can enliven your marriage and its own level of sensuality.

---

47. A desperate Michaela told our therapist that she had married someone who was "broken" during an early therapy session. We still laugh about the remark over twenty years later, but it was no laughing matter at the time.

By rebalancing daily priorities and moving romantic activities more to the forefront of our marriage, we have found our bond has strengthened and even intensified. We know yours will too.

Chapter 14

All Pathways

Evaluate the Implementation of Your Action Plans

Evaluation is at the heart of the six-pathway model. Evaluating oneself and one's marriage is a reflexive and continuous process. It can and should happen daily, during every pathway regardless of the order.

Continuous reflection has played a key role in our healing as a married couple. Reflexive techniques can help provide perspective not only on past challenges but also future opportunities. These opportunities may have mental health benefits: "Reminiscence and life review approaches can be directed toward preventing, assessing, and intervening with mental health problems of older adults" (Kunz, 2007, p. 164). For us, crafting my dissertation became an enormous and fulfilling reflexive project by which I was able to converse with various versions of myself over time through my journals and other primary data. When Michaela reviewed the draft, she cried in many parts because they reminded her of how far we have come.

To help identify challenges and opportunities in your marriage, consider the following action plan tool. The six pathways are listed on the left margin, and challenges, opportunities, and strategies are listed on top. Fill in any pathway at any point—you don't have to fill in everything or in a certain sequence. Consider a *specific* obsession-compulsion cycle that affects your marriage. What are the challenges that affect particular pathways? What opportunities could you as a married couple take advantage of to mitigate those challenges? Finally, what specific strategies could you employ to mitigate the challenges and facilitate the opportunities? You may find some helpful strategy suggestions in the preceding *action plans* for the pathways. Consider the example (Table 14.1) from our experience with scrupulosity, and use the template in Chapter 17 to create your own.

As a couple, you might have a child who you think struggles with traits of OCD. Developing an action plan for children dealing with overwhelming life events may help them better cope. First, invite them to develop a plan with you (see Table 14.1). Identify the challenges. Have children write these challenges down or draw them, or both. For me, challenges involved immediate things: new school, friends, teacher, and homework expectations. Help them consider opportunities farther on the horizon: other kids are having the same challenges, you'll overcome homework like you have in previous grades, you may end up liking this subject, etc. Finally, the therapeutic strategies could involve working with teaching aides on the subject, adjusting pedagogical approaches in the classroom, or working with friends who are dealing with some of the same challenges.

Table 14.1 (Page 107) This table represents a way we have approached the cycle of religious scrupulosity over several decades. The obsession was the fear my prayer was not perfect, ultimately resulting in our divorce, damnation, or some other sinister resolution. The compulsion was to not hold back and to pray spontaneously—in public or not—with my partner by placing my hands on top of her head, somehow 'perfecting' my prayer. Sometimes it would also mean I would try to say the same prayer for several minutes, restarting every time I messed up or something, like a bird, broke the silence. It was times like this that I wish I received a text from God: "It's OK."

Table 14.1

Action Plan—Public Scrupulosity

Pathway	Challenges	Opportunities	Strategies
ONE Cultivate Empathy	I know this is wrong, but I have to pray the perfect prayer, regardless of where I am. This cycle is all about me.	Listening to Michaela during therapy made me realize this affected her more than I realized.	• Actively participate in therapy • Meditate • Reflexive journaling
TWO Address Emotions	High emotional tag associated with saying prayers 'correctly'—but not sure why.	Identifying the emotional tags of scrupulosity can help me understand the irrational behavior that has humiliated my wife.	• Listen to Michaela's perspective • Journal empathically from her point of view • Find arts-based expression
THREE Improve Communications	Without warning, I place my hands on Michaela's head to pray in public places.	Actively listening to my partner helps me not take her for granted.	• Develop a phrase or word to signal a cycle: e.g., "You're doing it!" • The cycler has agreed previously to stop the cycle no matter what—this infers implicit trust.
FOUR Get Treatment	Years later, Michaela still is reluctant to pray with me.	Talking about our perspectives makes us feel heard and understand why we have behaved in certain ways.	• Conduct ERP to build up a tolerance to scrupulous obsessions • Discuss each other's perspectives. • Let the therapist mediate the next step.
FIVE Find Your Voices	I didn't listen to her during my cycling. I had to during therapy.	I can understand better why we pray differently—without judgment.	• Listen to each other's perspectives to allow each partner to feel heard. • Find an artistic way to express your emotions during/in response to this cycle.
SIX Rebalance & Romance	Although this hand-placing was a compulsion, it was a visible expression that I placed my scrupulosity ahead of her needs.	When we each feel valued in the relationship, we can celebrate our differences instead of letting them divide us. This celebration can draw us closer together.	• Don't force public prayers. • Lightly schedule private retreats—when she's ready. • Find virtual options (handy during pandemics!).

Synopsis

In this section, we have described the 6–Pathway Model, have examined the pathways and how they have applied to our marriage, have prompted you to consider how they would apply to your marital relationship, and have proposed some comprehensive strategies to confront OCD in your marriage. By evaluating these strategies from a holistic stance, you as a couple will build confidence together, in each other, to control OCD and strengthen your marriage.

Chapter 15
Interactive Exercises

Interactive Exercise 1:
Telling Your Own Story

Now that you have read our story, try starting your own. On the next page, in one—two clear, concise paragraphs, try to describe when and how you learned that you or a loved one had OCD. This is meant to be a free-writing exercise. Consider focusing on a particular experience that exemplifies your struggles with OCD. One way to organize your thoughts is by structuring them chronologically or by emotions experienced.[48] How did hearing the diagnosis make you feel? How did you physically respond to this new, significant information? How did you and your family make sense of it, or are you still struggling? Remember, you are not alone, and all affected families struggle with this disorder.

48. See Schmid, 2010, for more ideas.

When and how I learned that I or my loved one had OCD

Interactive Exercise 2:
Prayer

Meditative practices coupled with traditional therapies can positively affect OCD (Hofmann et al., 2011), thereby empowering individuals and marriages. Meditation can mean many things, but a common element in most traditions is that it involves deliberately seeking the undercurrent of love that permeates all life. One meditative approach I have found helpful in letting go of unwanted obsessive thoughts is Centering Prayer.

This method is contemplative because it entails my intentional consent to God's presence and transformative action within me. Put another way, I mindfully let go of my [OCD] ego and let God do the work needed to become my true self—to be open to love. This method complements my positionality as a lay Catholic contemplative in the Carmelite tradition. The method is also flexible to accommodate any faith practice simply by relabeling the action agent accordingly—e.g., God, Y-hw-h, Allah, Great Spirit, Mother Earth, etc. By adapting this contemplative method to your own identity and tradition, you can employ a powerful weapon against OCD.[49]

A centering prayer method I have used focuses on being grateful within a visual context. The first step is to select a word or short phrase that has a sacred meaning to you. It indicates something for which you are grateful, preferably no more than two syllables. For example, words such as Love, Health, God, Peace, and Serve are appropriate. Next, sitting in a comfortable and upright position, concentrate on breathing deeply and smoothly. You can close your eyes or keep them

---

49. Thomas Keating (1986/1992/2006) and Thomas Merton (1996) were trend-setting Christian spiritual masters who, as Trappist monks, opened many minds and hearts to the wisdom of other faith traditions. Both recognized that transformation starts from the Source within. Keating, in particular, revitalized the ancient contemplative practice he called Centering Prayer. The civil rights pioneer, John Lewis, had Merton's autobiography *The Seven Storey Mountain* (1948) in his knapsack during the 1965 march on Selma. For more information on Keating and Centering Prayer, check out the Contemplative Outreach site at www.contemplativeoutreach.org. The International Thomas Merton Society site at merton.org provides access to a comprehensive array of his works on various topics such as mysticism, social justice, and ecumenism.

open slightly, whatever offers the least distraction. Then, open your heart and mind. Sitting in silence for 15-20 minutes for perhaps twice daily, let thoughts come and go—like clouds flowing by on a spring day—and calmly say the sacred word to yourself when you need to come back to center. There's no need to try to stop the thoughts; just watch them pass by. At the end of the session, rest calmly for a minute or so, realizing you are more peaceful despite any disturbing thoughts or images you may have experienced.

To illustrate this method, I spent each of the forty days of Easter 2017 selecting a sacred word that represented what I was most grateful for. I then documented those words in a graphic that symbolized my unique faith identity and heritage: Celtic cross for Irish Catholicism, three Stars of David to represent the Carmelite crest and my Jewish heritage, and interconnected knots to represent the multi-layered complexities of my life (see Figure 15.1). On the fortieth day, I colored the symbol in pastels to link my artistic skills to the Easter season. I showed this graphic to my therapist who had suggested that I do something creative to represent my Easter prayer life. It offered her lots of information on my mental state over the time period, patterns of thought, and significant insights into my life experiences. Reflecting on the illustration provided a multi-faceted snapshot into my life at the time, making it a very powerful tool for facing my deep shadows and eliciting thankfulness.

In the space provided, consider drawing or selecting a graphic that symbolizes your life story. Follow the steps listed above and share it with your spouse and/or therapist. Better yet, do the exercise with your spouse. Represent the graphic in a way meaningful to you as an individual and couple. Reflect. Why did you choose the symbol? For what are you most thankful? What words repeat the most—if any—and what does that indicate? Are there any patterns? What have you learned about yourself and your marriage from this experience?

Figure 15.1
David's graphic of sacred words

Draw or select a graphic that symbolizes your life story. Follow the steps listed on Page 112 and share it with your spouse and/or therapist. Better yet, do the exercise with your spouse. Represent the graphic in a way meaningful to you as an individual and couple. Reflect. Why did you choose the symbol? For what are you most thankful? What words repeat the most—if any—and what does that indicate? Are there any patterns? What have you learned about yourself and your marriage from this experience?

Interactive Exercise 3:
Meditation

Meditative practices coupled with traditional therapies can positively affect OCD, thereby empowering individuals and marriages. Meditation can mean many things, but a common element in most traditions is that it involves mindfully seeking the undercurrent of love that permeates all life. One meditative approach I have found helpful in letting go of unwanted obsessive thoughts is breathing exercises. Less a methodology than a stance, this approach involves deliberately focusing on my breathing in a quiet place. Letting go of toxic thoughts in this manner can remind me that I'm not alone and can heal without harm.[50]

For this exercise, follow these steps:

1) Find a quiet place where you won't be disturbed for at least 15-20 minutes.

2) Get into a relaxed position in which you can breathe freely and not fall asleep.

3) Breathe in…. Breathe out… Try to 'see' the air go in and out of your lungs.

4) Keep your eyes closed to focus on an image or your breathing, or keep your eyes softly open—just avoid distractions.

5) If disruptive thoughts come into your mind, just focus back on your breathing.

6) Continue in this manner until your time is up.

7) Consider journaling about your experience (what you thought, how your body feels, etc.) to reflect on how to adjust your practice next time.

---

50. Hofmann et al. (2011) and Didonna (2020) discuss the use of mindfulness and meditative practices in OCD treatment. Keating (1986/1992/2006) was a Trappist monk who helped rejuvenate classical monastic contemplative practice in Centering Prayer. He helped found an organization, Contemplative Outreach, to spread the word about this simple, ancient approach to prayer. Please see Contemplative Outreach at www.contemplativeoutreach.org for more information about Centering Prayer and related programs.

Interactive Exercise 4:
Write Your Poem

Contemporary human-wide issues, such as the Corona Virus (COVID-19) pandemic in 2020-2021, have further stressed OCD-infused marriages. Despite the obvious challenges, there are some unique opportunities which married couples can create. The poem below describes some of our insights on self-authoring and creating learning opportunities from this devastating event. In the space after our poem, write your own. What does it say about how you have coped with OCD as a married couple? May you continue to create a stronger marriage despite OCD.

Figure 15.2

Cutting My Hair

I look into the COVID mirror,
And see my normal hair—nothing abnormal.
Little bit long around the ears, some sticking out my nose.
Old man tendrils. Nothing unusual.
Longest it's ever been.

My wife's camera says something else:
Feathers of a duck's tail winnowing down
Like a horse's mane—all hidden from reflection.
Waves of gray grass in a field of greasy filaments.
Blind to the reality...**hair needs trimming**.

Scissors on the desk, black and silver,
Challenge me to jump; take the next step
To stab her, to push her, to cheat with the 'handsome' woman—cycling, cycling.
No, to cut my hair!

I could stab, shove, shove, swerve, cheat, obliterate;
Escape, re-pray, or check the safety latch.
My hair is fine, but it needs shearing.
Now we both pick up the scissors,
Machined blades cool and objective,
Not caring which hair is struck.

Suddenly, the scissors take over,
Cycling through blades of grass to imprint
Perhaps a mullet or spike—not a trim.
I must stop it by touching the handles twice
And waiting 10 seconds. **You're welcome.**

We pick up the cutters again,
Telling them where to mow, hewing
The tree stumps and noxious weeds
So we can once more walk in the meadow,
Hand-in-hand leaning on each other
Wherever we want to go.
Peace, for now.

I place the scissors down on the countertop
And look in the mirror. **What next?**

Write your poem here: What have you achieved? What are your challenges? What are some opportunities? How has your relationship changed?

Some sources (and suggestions) you could consider include: triggers (Table 7.1), fears (Table 7.2), new vows (Figure 10.3), and/or life lessons (Figure 5.1).

Interactive Exercise 5:
How ready are you for positive change in your relationship?

Change. Changing behaviors is hard. Change when OCD is involved can be challenging at best. We have all tried to make positive changes in our lives, such as losing weight or quitting smoking. Positive changes can make us feel better about ourselves and our choices. How ready do you feel you and your partner are to tackle OCD in your relationship?

Changes in behavior do not happen quickly. In the 1970s, Prochaska and DiClemente conducted research on smoking cessation and developed a model that identifies and describes stages of change. Ultimately, they were trying to understand how some people could quit smoking on their own while others required additional treatment. They created the Stages of Change model based on human behaviors while going through a cycle of change.

The Stages of Change are defined in Table 15.1 that follows. As you look at the stages and their definitions, consider where you and your partner land in the cycle as you work together to build your relationship while changing behaviors to combat the effects of OCD in your relationship.

> **"Put up in a place where it is easy to see the cryptic admonishment: T.T.T.**
> **When you feel how depressingly slowly you climb, it's well to remember that Things Take Time."**
>
> – Piet Hein
> (1905-1996)

Table 15.1

The Stages of Change as as described by Prochaska et al. (1992)[51]

Stage	Definition	How to Move to the Next Stage
Precontemplation	In this stage, the individual is not ready to admit there is a problem behavior, therefore there is no need for change. People in this stage may have tried to make a change before but were unsuccessful.	Educate yourself on the benefits of the behavioral change. Think about the positive outcomes in your marriage because you worked on this particular behavior change.
Contemplation	The individual has knowledge of a problem behavior but is not ready or willing to make a change. In this stage, and individual weighs the benefits of the change with the barriers of making the change.	Identify the barriers to making positive change in your relationship. Identify concerns about making the change and identify people who can support the positive change. Identify the positive outcomes that result from making change.
Preparation	This stage focuses on the readiness to accept the need to change the problem behavior. In this stage, an individual is prepared to make small changes to behaviors.	Develop realistic goals and a timeline to meet the goals. Identify a person or people who can give you support as you work to achieve your goals.
Action	This is a stage of intentional action to change the behavior. The individual in this stage goes through the process of changing the problem behavior.	Renew your commitment to your goals and develop action plans that will help when the behaviors seem to relapse. Identify the positive changes that have happened and focus on the healthy behaviors that have emerged. Identify the long-term benefits of making this positive change.
Maintenance	This stage is about maintaining the positive behavior change.	Anticipate when the behaviors may re-emerge. Prepare strategies in advance that will assist when you feel the old behaviors are re-emerging.

51. See also www.adultmeducation.com/FacilitatingBehaviorChange.html which interprets the original model presented in Zimmerman, G., Olsen, C., & Bosworth, M. (2000). A 'Stages of Change' approach to helping patients change behavior. *American Family Physician*, 61(5), 1409-1416. www.aafp.org/afp/2000/0301/p1409.html

At the end of the day, you and your partner may be at different stages of the change cycle. It is important to remember that things take time. As we have written this book, we have wanted to make it clear that there will always be struggles. There are still days when David's obsessions and compulsions get on my very last nerve, and I know that is typical. What is important is how I react. I need to remember that my own happiness is important. If I'm not taking care of myself, then I cannot be supporting David to the best of my abilities. Healthy selfishness is important for my own well-being.

As a caregiver, it is OK to have a sense of healthy selfishness. This does not mean that your spouse's feelings do not matter. What it does mean is that we need to take care of ourselves, putting ourselves first.

1.   Is there a stumbling block in our relationship? What is the major stumbling block?

2.   Are we both ready to make positive changes? What are our ultimate goals? What steps can we take to meet our goals?

3. Is there someone in our lives who can be a support for us as we work towards common goals?

4. What are the long-term benefits that will result as we work towards our common goals? When you feel old behaviors re-emerge, how will you, as a couple, respond?

Section III

TOOLS &
RESOURCES

Key Objectives

This section intends to help you:

- use metaphors to understand OCD

- consider other ways to perceive OCD's influence in your marriage

- think of ways to use the tools presented to counter OCD in your marriage

- become aware of some OCD resources available

- get your family members involved in fighting OCD and strengthening your marriage

Chapter 16
Using Metaphors as a Way to Understand OCD

How often do we think we are headed in the right direction only to find out later that we were mistaken? I often feel this way when obsessive-compulsive cycles cloud my judgment. It can feel like I'm finishing a long race when, in truth, I have only crossed the finish line in the wrong direction. It can be a humbling experience. When we describe our experiences using language to illustrate how we make sense of the challenges we face, metaphors can be a helpful tool.

A metaphor is a linguistic tool that connects a concrete phenomenon experienced by our senses to an abstract concept that would be otherwise difficult to understand. Metaphors can help OCD sufferers and caregivers comprehend abstract expressions of obsessive-compulsive cycles and further interact with their personal stories in order to heal. Using metaphors to describe disturbing personal experiences can also enhance the therapist-participant relationship and therefore aid in collaboratively making sense of obsessive-compulsive patterns. In other words, metaphors can help us express our inner turbulence, so we can seek help and understanding. The following metaphors are but a few examples of how we have made sense of OCD in our relationship. What will work for you?[52]

We often use metaphors to help understand complex situations. As discussed in this book, OCD is a very complex phenomenon in any marriage. It can feel like, as Figure 16.1 depicts, running in the wrong direction even though—deep down—both partners know it's wrong. In this chapter, we'll examine how metaphors can help us describe complex experiences with OCD: self-centeredness, working with your partner, jumping to conclusions, and wearing masks to protect egos.

Figure 16.1
Going in the wrong direction

Metaphor 1:
Hand of Self-centeredness

Normally, people are pretty good taking their turn in life. Think of waiting in line at a grocery store or at a ballpark ticket line. There may be someone holding up the line who tests our patience, but (for the most part) we learn to live with it. After all, it could be us holding up the others for a variety of reasons. In class, we've been taught to raise our hand when we have a question and to lower it when we're permitted to speak. It's not about us; rather, it's about everyone getting the access they need to limited resources for the benefit of all.

When OCD enters the equation, this normal awareness of others' needs can become warped. An obsessive-compulsive cycle can become all-consuming, interrupting any mindful awareness of other's needs. In fact, the cycle itself can become an obsession. For example, when I am cycling and trying to listen to Michaela, it's as if my mind gums up and can only think of my obsessions. We have limited time to discuss our days, and I cannot wait any longer to tell her what I have to say. I can't ask her questions or have an adult conversation, because all I'm thinking about is the darned cycle. I can feel my blood pressure pound in my temples and almost immediately find myself in an impulsive "fight" posture—I cannot think, only act. So, what do I do? I compulsively raise my hand in a passive-aggressive way, selfishly interrupting her important point with, "When is it my turn? When can I talk?" In my mind, I've been waiting for several minutes to have a voice, so when I open my mouth, it's with a caustic and impatient tone. Not good for communication in any relationship.

Figure 16.2
The self-centeredness of OCD

When is my turn?

But we, as loving partners, can turn around our misperceptions represented by such metaphors. In this case, we can set boundaries and establish protocols to have truly collaborative and interactive conversations, not just briefing. Michaela and I have moved in this direction by first trusting that each of us has something valuable to say. When I'm cycling with an obsession, I need to have the courage to tell her, so she can give me some space and re-engage later. Now, we raise our hand to ask, "How are you?" The action no longer has a passive-aggressive tone but an empathetic one, further facilitating our communication.

OCD does not define a couple. It is a diagnosis of a mental disorder that becomes a "carry on" as the couple travels through life together. The following travel metaphor illustrates how OCD travels with a couple through life.

Figure 16.3

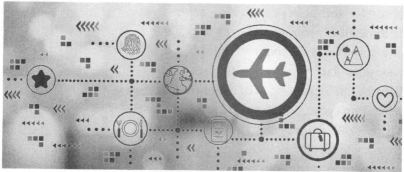

Metaphor 2:
Planning Your Trip—Packing Your Suitcase

We've all heard stories of how couples have met and fallen in love, and in many cases, eventually marry and travel through life together. Sometimes when we pack for a trip, we pack too much and have to set items aside in the last few hours before leaving home. David and I realized we both had baggage that we brought into the marriage. We soon realized that David had a lot of baggage that held us back, weighing on both of us and eventually dragging us down.

Realizing there was heavy baggage at the beginning of our trip together, we attempted to jettison some by going to a therapist to seek help. David had come to the false conclusion that I needed to know everything that he had experienced in life without me before we met. He felt that he had to tell me everything, no matter how small. He had come to the irrational conclusion that if he didn't tell me everything about his life growing up, we would be on the road to relationship disaster because he would have omitted things. The false premise was that omission equated with poor communication; poor communication would then result in distrust which would dissolve the marriage bond.

The result of this was the compulsion to write everything down that happened during his day while at work. Dave would arrive home every day with extra baggage, accompanied with a long list of phrases to help him remember to tell me things. This compulsion was his way of saving the marriage. The reality was we would spend up to an hour at the end of any workday consumed by a one-sided conversation without any interruptions permitted.

Checking In—Going Through Security

At this point, we had checked in for the trip. In other words, we were committed to a relationship with a no return policy on the tickets we had purchased. Divorce was not a viable option. We were going to make the relationship work, not realizing it was an uphill battle with an undiagnosed, invisible mental disorder that neither of us knew about.

As we learned more about each other and lived our vocation of marriage, we soon realized that something was not quite right. We experienced things that were atypical and seemed harmless. Dave would feel compelled to pray with his hands on my head, whether in private or public places. His brief lists became longer and more detailed, meaning telling me about his lists was taking longer. He had compulsions to tell me everything that went through his head, even if they should have remained "inside" thoughts. There were no filters since he felt if he didn't share everything with me, our marriage would be over. It felt like every time we went somewhere we were being slowed down, like going through the metal detector at an airport. Instead of using the background check that would allow us to go through airport security in the quick lane, we were always relegated to wait double the time for every trip, waiting in the long line to move forward.

At the Gate—Delayed

As a couple, we found ourselves delayed. The behaviors that manifested from the unknown presence of OCD held us back as David felt they became more and more necessary to present to alleviate the pestering obsessions in his head. This was not a pleasant time. Each obsession had a short-term solution by manifesting as a compulsion. As the partner, I had the choice to facilitate the obsessions or to "get on another flight." Either way, our relationship was on a delayed status. Summaries of David's day became longer and longer where I wasn't able to talk until the summary was over. Obsessions that were shared could be about anything, and often hurt me. This would lead to another obsession as he realized he had shared something that hurt me, and he shouldn't have thought about it in the first place. Our trip was delayed. We knew we needed help. We weren't enjoying life. We had come to a decision point -- a fork in the road.

Turbulence

We can both vividly remember our first trip together to the psychologist who would eventually diagnose David's OCD. We sat in the room together, ready to share our background with the psychologist, and all I could verbalize, to best describe our place at that moment, was to say, "He's so broken." We had experienced turbulence for such a long time, and that was the best way I could sum up everything. After a few sessions, we finally heard the diagnosis of OCD. It was like a weight off of our shoulders. The problem had been identified and now we could work on addressing it. We felt relieved. We could now feel safer in the turbulence because we had a seatbelt to keep us secure. We finally realized we weren't alone. Armed with a diagnosis, we could move on, no matter how turbulent the journey could be. We realized that others could help us to land our airplane safely.

We worked together to discover ways to make our relationship stronger. We continued our counseling sessions and did everything we could to research OCD. David continued to cycle through obsessive and intrusive thoughts, and we worked to build trust that when I said, "You're doing it," he was able to recalibrate and stop the cycle. This was not something that happened overnight, and we were committed to work together so the intrusive thoughts were not as loud in his head.

Landing

Once we landed with a diagnosis and our feet were on the ground, we were able to address deeper issues. We became more sensitive to people who had similar situations, and we have encouraged people to get past the social stigma of seeking help. Even though we landed with a diagnosis and ways to address OCD in our relationship, just like travel, there's always another "trip" or cycle to go through. With the support of family, friends, and God, we continue to work to build each other up and continue the journey of life together.

Prepping for the Next Leg

Our journey with OCD will never be over. Our choice to deal with a mental disorder in our relationship with love over anger has developed us as a couple and has made us stronger. We've learned to communicate more clearly with the ultimate goal of continued trust when dealing with OCD. We have learned to own the disorder instead of ignoring it. We work on being aware and open-minded, trying to stay away from hasty judgment.

Metaphor 3:
Filling Space and Jumping to Conclusions

How often have you judged yourself or your partner based upon limited information? I know I have. Usually, it results in an inaccurate conclusion that starts a heated conversation or, even worse, regrettable words. In groups, people fill up empty gaps of ignorance with assumptions that can turn into hurtful gossip. It's not a stretch of the imagination to conclude that jumping to conclusions based on incomplete, missing, or inaccurate information can harm relationships.

The mind is an amazing instrument of cognition and creativity. It routinely fills in gaps of knowledge by making assumptions that can later be corroborated or debunked. Linking objects to concepts and abstractions in the realm of creativity lends itself to metaphor but also possibly infers a connection to obsessive-compulsive rationalizations, disengaged from concrete reality (Wendler, 2017). This connectivity is apparent in the metaphor of a dotted picture in which individual points of various shades seemingly form intricate images when arranged in unique patterns.

Figure 16.4
The mind fills in the gaps

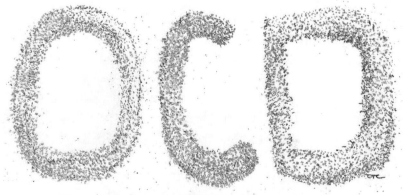

Illustration by D. Culkin, May 2020. How can our minds see each insignificant dot as part of a whole image?

Put another way, we can create false stories about ourselves and our partnerships when we don't bother to find out the facts that bear on our shared problems. Take a look at Figure 16.4. It actually is just a set of dots arranged on a page in such a way that our brains translate them as three separate letters. We appoint those dots a meaning that may or may not correspond with the artist's intention. The dots are like individual facts that our brains interpret by looking for patterns, differences, and gaps. When OCD cycles disrupt our thinking, it becomes harder to process facts. Our minds may feel "gummed up" with our cycles, preventing us from accurately translating the situation. For example, I may be so obsessed with germs that I constantly wash my hands and ritually enter rooms to ensure I remain safe. However, my "gummed up mind" may not even realize the irony of letting my outdoor dog lick my face when I return home. When OCD stymies our rational thoughts, it becomes harder for couples to identify and confront the disorder.

Metaphor 4:

Masks for Our Egos

We all wear figurative masks. A mask is anything that covers up our physical face or, symbolically, our egos. We tend to create such masks as we develop our identities in order to protect the person(s) we want to become.[53] We wear masks from youth. School children can present themselves as studious to their teachers—because they yearn for the recognition or fear their parents' wrath, or both—and lazy to their parents at home. Likewise, people with OCD have become experts in hiding their obsessions and compulsions, often in plain sight, in order to function in society.

Difficulties can arise when a couple's need to survive challenges the desires of the ego. An OCD sufferer may present herself as a

---

53. See David's dissertation and article summary to examine the role of masks in identity development over time (Culkin, 2016, 2019).

fastidious dresser in public because her ego, her idea of self, hinges upon people finding her physically attractive. At home with her partner, however, the beautiful mask can come off, revealing an insecure person who struggles with an eating disorder, unable to see her true self as a beautiful creation. Caregivers can accommodate their partners by wearing masks too. For example, the husband who puts on a smiling, patient face while facilitating another of his wife's compulsive cleaning rituals may cry in a closet after she goes to bed, distraught by how helpless he feels to stop her cycles and by how guilty he feels for thinking so.

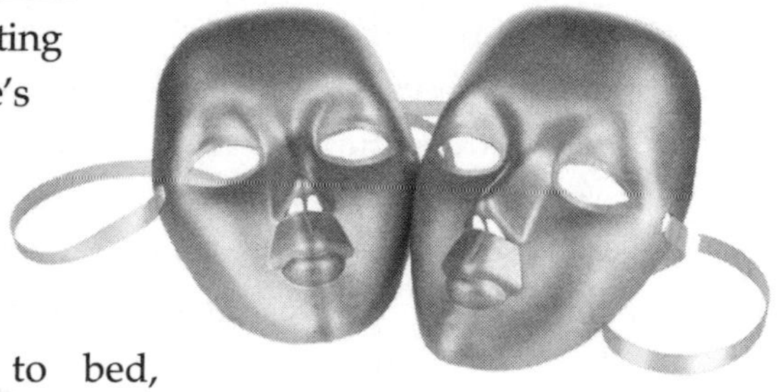

Figure 16.5

Spiritual masters of all faith traditions throughout the ages have posited that the life journey really involves shedding one's masks, to become their true selves.[54] They sometimes call such masks 'false selves,' masks we create to protect our egos. It can take years to shed some of the thickest masks in order to have a conversation with our true selves. Prayer, meditation, and therapy can all help couples shed these masks. What masks do you and your partner wear?

54. For more about false selves, see the References for Culkin, Keating, and Merton.

Discussion Questions

Use these questions to help focus group discussions and/or individual reflection on the entire book:

1. How can we, as a married team, manage OCD?

2. What are some strategies we can develop for an action plan?

3. What are the most important things we have learned about OCD and marriage?

4. Where can we find resources about OCD?

5. What metaphor best describes our marriage relationship?

6. How has the narrative of our relationship changed since we learned about OCD?

7. How can we rewrite our marriage story?

Synopsis

In this chapter, we have reviewed metaphor as a linguistic means to understand OCD and its effects on marital relationships. We presented a few metaphors to exemplify this concept. More importantly, we encourage you, as a married couple, to rewrite your story and thereby control the disorder's hold on your relationship.

Chapter 17
Putting it All Together

Obsessive-compulsive disorder (OCD) can have a very negative impact on any marriage, but it does not have to. That is the key message of this book. You and your spouse can take charge of obsessive-compulsive cycles that can syphon time, energy, and life out of a relationship, for both the afflicted and the caregiver. Since both partners are affected, it's usually best for both to actively participate in the remediation.

In previous chapters, we have discussed the nature of OCD in a marriage, how it has affected Michaela's and my relationship, and possible action plans to mitigate the negative effects of the disorder. A primary tool to control OCD in a marriage is the 6-Pathway Model by which a couple can iteratively address key issues (e.g., empathy, emotional intelligence, communication, treatment, finding voice, and balance) and then evaluate progress through action plans. Throughout the text, we have highlighted key areas of conflict or challenge with strategies grounded in current research. Furthermore, we have presented metaphors to help you better understand how OCD affects your marriage and then interactive exercises which you can implement for a comprehensive response to OCD. In this final chapter, some tools and resources are presented in one place to help you fight OCD and to strengthen your marriage.

Action Plan Template

An action plan is a primary OCD management tool that will help a married couple while undergoing professional treatment. As noted in chapters concerning the 6-Pathway Model, couples can organize action plans according to the model, or not—as they deem appropriate. They can use all or none of the pathways to organize their options, at any level of detail. The key is that they plan to act and follow through on the strategies to overcome challenges and exploit opportunities. Table 17.1 on the next page is a template for an action plan organized around the 6-pathways. Table 14.1, noted earlier, represents a completed plan for comparison. After an agreed-upon period, evaluate how well you, as a couple, accomplished each strategy. Identify reasons why certain challenges remain or particular opportunities are still out of reach. Do you need to adjust some of the strategies? Why? How?

Table 17.1
Action Plan—Template

Pathway	Challenges	Opportunities	Strategies
ONE Cultivate Empathy			• • •
TWO Address Emotions			• • •
THREE Improve Communications			• •
FOUR Get Treatment			• • •
FIVE Find Your Voices			• •
SIX Rebalance & Romance			• • •

Format for a Learning Audit

A learning audit is an educational assessment tool popular in many adult learning environments. It is a systematic way to identify strengths and weaknesses of learning programs and activities through active questioning.[55] For the purposes of determining if a married couple is on track with their action plan, an audit may be as simple as answering a series of questions in a journal for each strategy.

Sharing your answers with each other and your therapist can elicit deep conversations (Pathway Four) that can help you better grasp:

(Pathway One), empathy

(Pathway Two), emotions

(Pathway Three), communications

(Pathway Five), identity

(Pathway Six), loving balance

- What have we learned about OCD that we didn't know before?

- What is the most important thing we have learned by executing this action plan?

- What is still confusing about this strategy?

- What or who helped us better understand OCD? How?

55. Brookfield, 2006; Thalheimer, 2017.

Therapies and Medications

Mental health researchers and providers have introduced several therapies and medications for OCD in recent decades. While this book is not a medical text that provides prescriptive advice, we attempt to identify some of the more common tools available to married couples struggling with the disorder. We'll discuss when they're appropriate, questions to ask the experts, and the importance of taking responsibility for your own treatment.

These therapeutic approaches aim to identify and correct troublesome cognitions or thought patterns that spark obsessions and stimulate compulsive behaviors.

Most therapies and medications have become well-accepted in the mental health community because they complement each other and are adaptable. Medications and therapy together treat OCD, and it should be noted that while OCD does not have a cure, it can be managed. Cognitive-behavioral therapy (CBT) has become the gold standard of therapy strategies. It has become an umbrella for a variety of approaches that target aspects of OCD: exposure and response prevention, mindfulness, and acceptance and commitment. These therapeutic approaches aim to identify and correct troublesome cognitions or thought patterns that spark obsessions and stimulate compulsive behaviors.

Several references describe these techniques in detail. Jonathan Abramowitz's *Getting Over OCD* (2018) is particularly useful because he lays out practical steps to challenge problematic cognitive patterns through worksheets and interactive activities. His workbook is a readable place to start researching your options when you are newly diagnosed. He clearly lays out how serotonin-specific reuptake inhibitors (SSRI) such as Zoloft, Luvox, Prozac, and Paxil are some of the most common medications prescribed to complement CBT. That said, current research does not clearly indicate whether the chemical imbalance of neurotransmitters such as serotonin, unique brain anatomy, or learning environments cause OCD (Abramowitz, 2018). David Clark's *Cognitive-Behavioral Therapy for OCD and its Subtypes* (2020) is an excellent resource for survivors and therapists who seek to understand OCD diagnosis, theory, and relationships at a deeper level. These and other references don't replace finding your own motivation to find professional help and ask probing questions.

It's most appropriate to seek these therapies and medications when you decide, in collaboration with your mental health provider(s), it's best for you and your family. Realizing something is wrong or "off" in a marriage may be relatively straightforward, but describing the cause and indicators can be a significant challenge. Michaela and I knew something was off by the second year of our marriage, but we didn't get a diagnosis that explained what was causing our disorder until the seventh year. When you get to the point that it's either the marriage or seeking help, it is time to make an appointment with a professional health care provider.

One of the key ways to learn about OCD treatments and to take responsibility for your treatment is by asking questions of reliable experts. Not all health care providers are equally trained to address the challenges of OCD in marriages. Licensed counselors, social workers, and clinical therapists often have the credentials, but you need to meet them to ensure the "fit" is mutual. We tried a support group and an OCD-trained counselor before settling on a therapist that worked for us. Every couple is different because its individual members are unique people with different beliefs, values, and perspectives. Likewise, therapists are unique in their approaches to and understanding of OCD. We often found we knew more about

OCD and its symptoms than our primary care providers who referred us to mental health professionals.[56]

Find the best therapist or counselor for you.

Take the time and gumption to interview potential providers first. It really is a job selection process because whom you pick could potentially save your marriage. Some questions that we have found helpful are:

- What is your experience in providing therapy for OCD?

- Why are you motivated to help married couples with OCD?

- How long have you provided therapy to couples with OCD and related disorders?

- What treatment resources (i.e., workbooks, activities, support communities) do you use?

- What is the role of medications, in your professional opinion, for OCD treatment?

- What would you recommend if your son or daughter was in our situation?

As a result, we found that a qualified provider was someone who was open to learn about the disorder with us, use current resources to structure treatment, and foster our motivation to improve ourselves and our relationship.

To be clear, taking responsibility for your own treatment is crucial because you are the direct beneficiary of its efficacy. Nothing is accomplished when we blame others for our predicament. We must discern when it is appropriate to seek professional help and ask probing questions to find the best fitting health care provider.

---

56. For example, when I was a pilot my employer stipulated that I had to be asymptomatic after being off medications for a year in order to resume flight duties. My reality was that I would likely remain on medications for the rest of my life. This policy ignored the fact that there is no cure for OCD, despite available treatments.

CBT and Multimodal Therapy

There have been times that I felt I knew more about OCD than the clinician counseling me or the person writing a prescription for a medication such as a serotonin-specific reuptake inhibitor (SSRI). Perhaps I was more motivated to learn about a disorder that has had a serious impact on my married life. Perhaps there's little reason to focus on a disorder in psychiatric training when it only affects 2.2 million adults in the United States—approximately one percent of the population.[57] That said, it was disconcerting when a physician told me had perfectionistic traits too, that he somehow knew what my wife and I were going through. I also remember explaining to a counselor who had received specialized OCD training in a workshop that my anxieties were rooted in taboo-related obsessions concerning sexuality, religion, and violence. He didn't understand that my compulsions were mostly 'in my head' and I wouldn't act them out, but they were just as toxic to the relationship as physical behaviors.

Cognitive-behavioral therapy (CBT) has been the baseline for OCD treatment since the 1960s. Unlike other forms of therapy that focus on dialogue between the patient and clinician (e.g., psychoanalysis), CBT focuses on actions. Providers will commonly coach patients to learn new skills such as exposure and response prevention (ERP).[58] Modifying how we think about what we think (i.e., metacognition) can influence how we behaviorally respond to our thoughts.

In this section, we'll take a deeper look at cognitive-behavioral therapy (CBT) which has become the gold standard of therapies for OCD. First, we'll consider some of the variables clinicians consider when diagnosing the disorder and prescribing medications. Next, we'll describe five basic techniques commonly used for CBT and

57. The Anxiety and Depression Association of America (ADAA) website at https://adaa.org/understanding-anxiety/facts-statistics#:~:text=OCD%20affects%202.2%20million%20adults,cases%20occurring%20by%20age%2014. Retrieved on 25 April, 2021.
58. See Abramowitz, 2018.

multiple approaches (multimodal) to OCD therapy that have arisen in recent decades. Finally, we'll summarize some key advantages and disadvantages to getting CBT in a cost-benefit analysis table.[59]

Variables of Diagnosis and Treatment

While we are not medical professionals who can provide health advice, we can speak from our own experiences of diagnosis, prescription, and therapy with a unique point of view: patient and caregiver. Several of these variables may factor into a clinician's judgments. Knowing about these variables can make you better informed and facilitate self-advocacy.

Intensity

First, the *intensity* of your obsessions and compulsive cycles can indicate how ingrained OCD is in your patterns of thought. If your husband spends hours every night ritually cleaning himself and the bathroom, he—and you—will likely have little time for much else. Avoiding triggers, accommodating compulsions, or even acknowledging the legitimacy of such behaviors can cement such obsession-compulsion cycles over time. The longer the time period, the harder it may seem to break the cycles. For this reason, intensity often corresponds to duration.

Duration

Duration refers to the overall time period a person has experienced particular obsession-compulsion cycles. Each cycle may be only a few minutes or several hours. Regardless, the repetition of such cycles tends to reinforce their cognitive

---

59. To learn more about CBT for OCD and related disorders, check out Exposure therapy for anxiety (Abramowitz et al., 2019, Chapter 23) and Cognitive-behavioral therapy for OCD and its subtypes (Clark, 2020, Figure 4.1). Both sources provide content discussed in this section; they also provide detailed analysis of each technique.

and behavioral habits. Research does not conclusively find that OCD is caused by specific brain anatomy or neurochemical imbalances (Abramowitz, 2018). There is still a lot to learn about the disorder, but patients and caregivers alike know very well the pain and disruption it can cause.

Comorbidity

Like many phenomena in life, OCD often does not happen in isolation. A couple could experience the simultaneous occurrence of two or more disorders in one partner. Such *comorbidity* in OCD patients is rather common with some other disorders: depression, anxiety, OCD spectrum disorders such as body dysmorphic disorder (BDD) and trichotillomania (TTM), tics, psychosis, substance abuse, and personality disorders. Some disorders, such as depression, may increase the degree of a person's impairment; but research still has a way to go to link the severity of certain disorders with positive treatment outcomes.[60]

Frequency

Another variable that can play a role in diagnosis and treatment is *frequency*. Frequency is a measure of repeated events within a particular window of time. A person with OCD could experience recurring intrusive thoughts that persist and intensify over time. Some clinicians who have not experienced OCD themselves may focus on the objective measure of such cycles. For example, a patient who experiences thoughts of molesting young children could record every time he has such thoughts. This data would certainly help identify the frequency of the thoughts, but the patient can also experience another dimension of these thoughts not captured by empirical measures. The same

---

60. See Clark (2020, Chapter 1) for a detailed explanation of OCD and comorbidity.

patient may further cement a conviction that he is an incurable pedophile because of the occurrence of these thoughts. Somehow the existence of the thoughts indicates his possible identity as a social deviant. Of course, no fax will come from Heaven to confirm the person's identity. Measuring the frequency can reinforce that conviction that he is a pedophile—despite having never acted out on such thoughts.

These variables can help clinicians and researchers better understand OCD in their patients and participants; but the variables sometimes fail to tell the internal, immeasurable toll the disorder can have on identity, self-worth, and relationships. Often, listening to the stories of pain and survival told by patients and caregivers can have a significant healing effect, enabling everyone involved to learn more about themselves and the disorder.[61]

Five CBT and Multimodal Techniques for OCD

Multimodal approaches to OCD treatment normally consist of medication, couples counseling, psychoeducation, and cognitive-behavioral therapy (CBT) with exposure and response prevention (ERP) in particular. As discussed earlier, medications tend to be systemic and may address alleged chemical imbalances in the brain. Couples counseling is a great way to foster communication in a relationship while surviving OCD, but many partners—sadly—don't see a need to participate. After all, "I'm not the one who has OCD." That attitude could not be farther from the truth. What affects one partner in a marriage affects the whole relationship. Changing such attitudes is one object of psychoeducation because it then enables therapeutic intervention. Finally, CBT with ERP, when proctored in controlled and supervised programs of treatment, can help desensitize patients to stimuli and allow them to realize that nothing

---

61. For more on healing from OCD through telling, listening to, and retelling stories, see Culkin (2016, 2019) and Weg (2011).

bad will happen as a consequence of not carrying out compulsion in response to obsessions.[62]

Essentially, ERP exposes sufferers to the triggers of their obsessions and encourages them to desist from doing compulsive rituals (response prevention) that offer temporary relief. When patients eventually see that they survive the obsessions, fears, and anxiety from not performing the compulsions, they can begin to adjust their misperceptions. Based on this foundation, there are five basic techniques of CBT for OCD treatment:[63]

Technique 1
Actual Exposure to Triggers

A common approach to exposure therapy is getting close to the actual thoughts, patterns, or situations that can stimulate the obsessions. This type of therapy is situational in that it places the patient in particular conditions that trigger the troublesome thoughts (Abramowitz, 2018). For instance, a woman with germophobic obsessions could, under a controlled environment, expose herself to the 'unclean' environment to activate her obsessions but stop short of performing her compulsive cleaning rituals. Physical rituals that have limited risk of harm to self or others can often be treated quite effectively through situational exposure.

Technique 2
Imaginary Exposure

Of course, it may not always be possible to simulate such triggers in therapy. Consider the man who obsessively fears he may stab his wife every time he handles a knife in the kitchen. Holding a knife in her presence may not only be disturbing for her but also put undue distress on him. In this case, an imaginary exposure may be

---

62. Abramowitz et al. (2019, p. 354) discusses medications in greater detail. Clark (2020, pp. 92 & 203) describes how psychoeducation can promote successful therapies in multimodal contexts.
63. Check out a table that lays out CBT techniques and their purposes and goals (Abramowitz, 2018, p. 89).

appropriate. For example, he could record himself describing in detail a situation in which he holds the knife in her presence and carries the obsessional cycle through, only to realize the resultant anxiety doesn't correspond with him carrying out any violent act. My wife once told me that I worried about things I wouldn't do, and there are psychopaths out there who don't care about what they've done. Research findings indicate that situational and imaginary exposure techniques can be relatively effective in addressing 'sticky' obsession-compulsion cycles.[64]

Technique 3
Response Prevention

Response prevention, mentioned previously, assumes that patients can habituate or become desensitized to stimuli that trigger obsessions.[65] Key elements in this therapy include pre-planned exposure situations, assessing before-after sessions with trained care providers, psychoeducation, and prioritizing obsessions that cause great anxiety levels. If a person experiences many obsession-compulsion cycles, it can help to focus on a select few to begin.

Technique 4
Cognitive Therapy

Cognitive therapy focuses on correcting thought patterns built upon misperceptions and faulty logic. It centers on identifying and analyzing obsessional thoughts when they occur and being open to correcting them. In marriages, partners can also point out when their loved one is obsessing or begins 'to cycle.' In these circumstances, it can take quite a while to attain a level of trust in which a person with OCD can willingly respond to their partner's alarm: "Hey, you're doing it again!"

---

64. See Abramowitz et al. (2019, p. 25).
65. See Abramowitz (2018) and Clark (2020) for more information on exposure and response prevention for OCD treatment.

Technique 5
Acceptance and Commitment Therapy (ACT)

Just like cognitive therapy, ACT appeals to open mindedness toward obsessional thinking patterns. A patient will try to acknowledge when she compulsively avoids triggers and attempt to think about obsessions, doubt, and uncertainty in a different way. Rather than fighting and ignoring obsessions and intrusive thought cycles, patients using ACT will try to cope better with them. In this sense, the patient embraces the problem of obsessive thoughts rather than run away from them.

Cost-Benefit Analysis of CBT for OCD

In this section, we examined three aspects of cognitive-behavioral therapy (CBT) which has become the standard therapy for OCD. First, we described some variables clinicians consider when diagnosing the disorder and prescribing medications. Next, we looked at five basic techniques commonly used for CBT and multiple approaches (multimodal) to OCD therapy. Table 17.2 summarizes some key advantages and disadvantages of getting CBT (based on these five CBT techniques) in a cost-benefit analysis table that could structure an initial conversation with a new therapist.[66]

---

66. Other references that describe the advantages and disadvantages of CBT for OCD is Exposure therapy for anxiety (Abramowitz et al., 2019, Chapter 23) and Clark's Cognitive-behavioral therapy for OCD and its subtypes (2020, Figure 4.1, p. 91) which focuses on the costs-benefits of ERP.

Table 17.2

Treatment for OCD	Benefits / Advantages	Costs / Disadvantages
With CBT	• Gold-standard treatment • Backed by empirical research • Situational and imaginary exposure especially effective • Involves the partner and family in treatment plans • Practice life skills to cope with OCD	• Exposure can cause distress • Involves considerable investment of time and energy • Needs both partners to be successful in the long-term • Can trigger doubts and uncertainties in the short term
Without CBT	• Avoids short-term distress with exposure • Skips costs associated with professional treatment	• Undue stress on relationship, possibly leading to separation or divorce • Continued misperceptions of reality • Unhappiness for both partners • Avoidance and accommodations continue

OCD Support Organizations

Several community and clinical organizations offer resources and services for married couples with obsessive-compulsive disorder (OCD). There are many online resources such as apps, podcasts, and videos of various quality and currency. We recommend you start with the websites of two professional organizations that have established track records of supporting patients, family members, therapists, and researchers.

The International Obsessive-Compulsive Disorder Foundation (IOCDF, 2020)
iocdf.org
Is dedicated to improving the lives and families of those affected by OCD. Currently, it is the only international non-profit organization that regularly organizes conferences, web-education, fundraisers, and community events in support of OCD-related research and resources. It aims to build local and national collaborative communities not only among sufferers but also caregivers, clinicians, and researchers.

Anxiety and Depression Association of America (ADAA, 2020)
adaa.org

Like the IOCDF site, it provides information on various related aspects of the disorder, including: teenage symptoms, health care providers, hoarding, Tourette's Syndrome, and body dysmorphic disorder (BDD).

Other websites offer a tremendous amount of resources and suggestions.

BeyondOCD.org

A one-stop website for both sufferers and caretakers of OCD. Started in 2018, this tool both defines OCD and gives practical suggestions for various therapies in a user-friendly format.

OCDandMarriage.com
Reshape Your Lives Together

You may also find our website as a helpful reference. We have tried to make our book accessible and provide a safe space for people coping with this disorder to have their voices heard.

Help is available

You owe it to your marriage and family to seek help and apply tools that are appropriate to your life circumstances. Having a discussion with your therapist on the pros/cons of certain options can help you prioritize what you want to get out of your time using them. These prompts may assist you in a conversation to identify which tool(s) would help your marriage in dealing with OCD:

- What type of tool (e.g., therapy group, app, workbook, etc.) would be most effective to cope with OCD in our marriage?
- How should we use this tool(s)—time commitment, frequency, together or alone, et cetera?
- Should we share our experiences with each other? With the therapist?
- How do we know when we are improving? How can we, as a married couple, better handle OCD?

Literature and Resources

While there is a lot of material about OCD, few of the current resources address the topic from a survivor's point-of-view, particularly regarding the effects of OCD on marriage. Orlov's (2010, 2014) texts on ADHD provide a well-known framework from which we can derive and further develop a viable coping strategy for married couples contending with OCD. Additionally, this book addresses living with the disorder on a daily basis from survivors' experiences rather than from a clinician's perspective that—for very good reasons—must restrain certain details to protect patient confidentiality. This book can also serve as a tool therapists can use with married patients who want to fight OCD as a couple in a holistic and proactive way. Because we tell our stories covering several decades of living with the disorder in different ways, *OCD and Marriage* is meant to assist married couples struggling with OCD at various points in their life course.

Current texts in the market are well established and have personally helped our relationship survive:

Abramowitz, J. S. (2021). *The family guide to getting over OCD: Reclaim your life and help your loved one.* The Guilford Press.

Bourne, E. J. (1995). *The anxiety and phobia workbook* (2nd ed.). New Harbinger Publications, Inc.

Didonna, F. (2020). *Mindfulness-based cognitive therapy for OCD: A treatment manual.* The Guilford Press.

Hyman, B. M., & Pedrick, C. (1999). *The OCD workbook: Your guide to breaking free from Obsessive-Compulsive Disorder.* New Harbinger Publications, Inc.

Orlov, M. (2010). *The ADHD effect on marriage: Understand and rebuild your relationship in six steps.* Specialty Press, Inc.

Orlov, M., & Kohlenberger, N. (2014). *The couple's guide to thriving with ADHD.* Specialty Press, Inc.

Weg, A. H. (2011). *OCD treatment through storytelling: A strategy for successful therapy.* Oxford University Press.

For information about OCD and children we recommend the following resources:

Zucker, B (2021). *Take control of ocd: A kid's guide to conquering anxiety and managing ocd.* Prufrock Press.

Zucker, B (2016). *Anxiety-free kids: Interactive for parents and children.* Prufrock Press.

Concluding Thoughts

In this book we convey a simple message: married couples coping with OCD can self-author their healing and relationships. Our intent has not been to reiterate clinical advice already widely available; rather, we hope we have shared our life story of OCD survival with other married couples whom, until now, resources have not specifically targeted.

We have organized the chapters into three sections to describe our personal experiences, provide a model to rebuild your marriage within the context of OCD survival, and offer some tools and resources to help you on your continued journey. Section I focused on understanding the basics of OCD related to marriage and mindful awareness. Section II presented a modification of Orlov's 6-Pathway Model to rebuild a marriage marred by the disorder. Each pathway was described, illustrated with our personal examples. This holistic, integrated approach involves a continuous evaluation of progress. Setbacks are normal, but a resilient couple can anticipate them and bounce back. Section III presented some metaphors to help a couple visualize and thereby better understand and express how OCD affects its relationship. This section also examined how a couple can employ available tools and resources to develop and implement action plans to take control of OCD in a marriage. Throughout, we have provided specific vignettes of our personal stories, related implications from current research, and suggested interactive exercises to apply key concepts to your own marriage. We wish you the best on your journey together.

References

Abramowitz, J. S. (2018). *Getting over OCD: A 10-step workbook for taking back your life* (2nd ed.). The Guilford Press.

Abramowitz, J. S. (2021). *The family guide to getting over OCD: Reclaim your life and help your loved one.* The Guilford Press.

Abramowitz, J. S., Deacon, B. J., & Whiteside, S. P. H. (2019). *Exposure therapy for anxiety: Principles and practice* (2nd ed.). The Guilford Press.

American Psychiatric Association (APA). (2013a). *Diagnostic and statistical manual of mental disorders* (5th ed.). American Psychiatric Publishing.

American Psychiatric Association (APA). (2013b). *Obsessive compulsive and related disorders.* Washington, DC. Retrieved on 29 August 2019 at https://www.psychiatry.org/File%20Library/Psychiatrists/Practice/DSM/APA_DSM-5-Obsessive-Compulsive-Disorder.pdf

Anxiety and Depression Association of America (ADAA). (2020, April 24). *OCD.* https://adaa.org/understanding-anxiety/obsessive-compulsive-disorder-ocd

Baldacchino, R. V., & Baldacchino, J. V. (2016). From hero to zero: The manifestation of addictive problematic sexual behavior [Synopsis]. 24th European Congress of Psychiatry / *European Psychiatry, 33S,* S592. http://dx.doi.org/10.1016/j.eurpsy.2016.01.2206

Baer, L. (2002). *The imp of the mind: Exploring the silent epidemic of obsessive bad thoughts.* Plume.

Baumgardner, J. (2017, August 16). *Keys to effective communication in marriage*. First Things First. https://firstthings.org/keys-to-effective-communication-in-marriage/

Beverley, J. A. (2004/2008). *Creating loving relationships: Living a life of authenticity*. Aurora Canyon Publishing.

Beyond OCD. (2021, April 11). About us. https://beyondocd.org/

Brookfield, S. (2006). *The skillful teacher: On technique, trust, and responsiveness in the classroom* (2nd ed.). Jossey-Bass.

Brooks, J. (Director). (1997). *As good as it gets* [Film]. TriStar Pictures.

Brown, N. (2001). *Children of the self-absorbed: A grownup's guide to getting over narcissistic parents*. New Harbinger Publications, Inc.

Clark, D. A. (2020). *Cognitive-behavioral therapy for OCD and its subtypes* (2nd ed.). The Guilford Press.

Clark, D. A., & O'Connor, K. (2005). *Thinking is believing: Ego-dystonic intrusive thoughts in Obsessive-Compulsive Disorder*. In D. Clark (Ed.), *Intrusive thoughts in clinical disorders: Theory, research, and treatment* (pp. 145-174). The Guilford Press.

Clark, D. A., & Rhyno, S. (2005). Unwanted intrusive thoughts in nonclinical individuals: Implications for clinical disorders. In D. Clark (Ed.), *Intrusive thoughts in clinical disorders: Theory, research, and treatment* (pp. 1-29). The Guilford Press.

Coimbra-Gomes, E., & Motschenbacher, H. (2019). Language, normativity, and sexual orientation obsessive-compulsive disorder (SO-OCD): A corpus-assisted discourse analysis. *Language in Society, 48*(4), 565-584. 10.1017/S0047404519000423

Covey, S., & Merrill, R. (2006). *The speed of trust: The one thing that changes everything*. Free Press.

Culkin, D. (2016). *A need to heal: An autoethnographic bildungsroman through the shadows* (Doctoral dissertation). Retrieved from K-Rex at https://krex.k-state.edu/dspace/handle/2097/34454

Culkin, D. (2019). A need to continue healing: Report of findings from an autoethnographic study. *The Qualitative Report, 24*(12), 3150-3191. https://doi.org/10.46743/2160-3715/2019.3966

Didonna, F. (2020). *Mindfulness-based cognitive therapy for OCD: A treatment manual.* The Guilford Press.

Hofmann, S., Grossman, P., & Hinton, D. (2011). Loving-kindness and compassion meditation: Potential for psychological interventions. *Clinical Psychology Review, 31,* 1126-1132. 10.1016/j.cpr.2011.07.003

Hyman, B., & Pedrick, C. (1999). *The OCD workbook: Your guide to breaking free from Obsessive-Compulsive Disorder.* New Harbinger Publications, Inc.

International Obsessive-Compulsive Disorder Foundation (IOCDF). (2020, April 24). Home page. https://iocdf.org/

Keating, T. (1986/1992/2006). *Open mind, open heart: The contemplative dimension of the Gospel* (20th anniversary ed.). Bloomsbury.

Knapton, O., & Rundblad, G. (2018). Metaphor, discourse dynamics and register: Applications to written descriptions of mental health problems. *Text & Talk, 38* (3), 389-410. https://doi.org/10.1515/text-2018-0005

Koen, N., & Stein, D. (2015). Obsessive-compulsive disorder. In M. Zigmond, L. Rowland & J. Coyle (Eds.), *Neurobiology of brain disorders: Biological basis of neurological and psychiatric disorders* (pp. 621-638). Academic Press.

Kunz, J. (2007). Mental health applications of reminiscence and life review. In J. Kunz & F. Soltys (Eds.), *Transformational reminiscence: Life story work* (pp. 155-180). Springer Publishing Company, LLC.

May, Gerald. (2004). *The dark night of the soul: A psychiatrist explores the connection between darkness and spiritual growth.* HarperOne.

Merton, T. (1996). *Contemplative prayer.* Doubleday.

Minelli, A., & Maffioletti, E. (2014). Genetics of anxiety disorders. In S. Roman (Ed.), *Anxiety disorders: Risk factors, genetic determinants and cognitive-behavioral treatment* (pp. 67-92). Novinka.

Orlov, M. (2010). *The ADHD effect on marriage: Understand and rebuild your relationship in six steps.* Specialty Press, Inc.

Orlov, M., & Kohlenberger, N. (2014). *The couple's guide to thriving with ADHD*. Specialty Press, Inc.

Oz, F. (Director). (1991). *What about Bob?* [Film]. Touchstone Pictures.

Paradiso-Michau, M. (2018). Empathy and the face: Edith Stein and Emmanuel Levinas. In K. Haney (Ed.), *Listening to Edith Stein: wisdom for a new century* (Carmelite Studies 12, pp. 267-283). ICS Publications.

Patel, S., Wheaton, M., Andersson, E., Ruck, C., Schmidt, A., Lima, C., Galfavy, H., Pascucci, O., Myers, R., Dixon, L., & Simpson, H. (2018). Acceptability, feasibility, and effectiveness of internet-based cognitive-behavioral therapy for obsessive-compulsive disorder in New York. *Behavior Therapy, 49*, 631-641.

Prochaska, J., DiClemente, C., & Norcross, J. (1992). In search of how people change: Applications to the addictive behaviors. *American Psychologist, 47*(9), 1102-1114. doi: 10.1037//0003-066x.47.9.1102

Roncero, M., Belloch, A., & Doron, G. (2018). A novel approach to challenging OCD related beliefs using a mobile-app: An exploratory study. *Journal of behavior therapy and experimental psychiatry, 59*, 157-160. https://doi.org/10.1016/j.jbtep.2018.01.008

Samantaray, N., Kar, N., & Singh, P. (2019). Four-session cognitive behavioral therapy for the management of obsessive-compulsive disorder using a metaphor for conceptualization: A case report. *Indian Journal of Psychiatry, 61* (4), 424.

Schmid, W. (2010). *Narratology: An introduction*. De Gruyter.

Schwandt, T. (2015). *The Sage Dictionary of Qualitative Inquiry* (4th ed.). Sage.

Schwartz, J., & Beyette, B. (1996/2016). *Brain lock: Free yourself from obsessive-compulsive behavior* (20th Anniversary ed.). Harper Perennial.

Steketee, G., & Van Noppen, B. (2004). Family approaches to treatment for Obsessive Compulsive Disorder. *Journal of Family Psychotherapy, 14*(4), 55-71. 10.1300/J085v14n04_06

Strauss, A., Huppert, J., Simpson, H., & Foa, E. (2018). What matters more? Common or specific factors in cognitive behavioral therapy for OCD: Therapeutic alliance and expectations as predictors of treatment outcome. *Behaviour Research and Therapy, 105*, 43-51. https://doi.org/10.1016/j.brat.2018.03.007

Tang, H., Chen, P., & Lung, F. (2018). Personality and alexithymic disparity in Obsessive-Compulsive Disorder based on washing and checking. *Psychiatric Quarterly, 89*(2), 371-381. 10.1007/s11126-017-9541-8

Thalheimer, W. (2017). How to conduct a learning audit. *Work-Learning Research*, 1-23. https://www.worklearning.com/wp-content/uploads/2017/10/How-to-Conduct-a-Learning-Audit.pdf

Thompson, F. (1917). *The hound of heaven* [Poem]. In D. Nicholson & A. Lee (Eds.), *The Oxford Book of English Mystical Verse*. The Clarendon Press, 1917; Bartleby.com, 2000. www.bartleby.com/236/ [2020, May 6].

Tolle, E. (1999/2010). *The power of now: A guide to spiritual enlightenment.* New World Publishing.

Weg, A. H. (2011). *OCD Treatment through storytelling: A strategy for successful therapy.* Oxford University Press.

Wendler, E. (2017). Leakings, drafts and magical thinking: Synaesthesia, creativity and Obsessive-Compulsive Disorder—Is there a link? *The Journal of Transpersonal Psychology, 49* (2), 136-148.

Index